AF600078

THE NATURE OF SUPPORT OF DIOCESAN PRIESTS IN THE UNITED STATES OF AMERICA

THE CATHOLIC UNIVERSITY OF AMERICA
CANON LAW STUDIES

No. 286

THE NATURE OF SUPPORT OF DIOCESAN PRIESTS IN THE UNITED STATES OF AMERICA

A HISTORICAL SYNOPSIS
AND A COMMENTARY

BY

REV. KENNETH R. O'BRIEN, A.B., J.C.L.
Priest of the Archdiocese of Los Angeles

A DISSERTATION

Submitted to the Faculty of the School of Canon Law of the Catholic University of America in Partial Fulfillment of the Requirements for the Degree of Doctor of Canon Law

THE CATHOLIC UNIVERSITY OF AMERICA PRESS
WASHINGTON, D.C.
1949

NIHIL OBSTAT

HIERONYMUS D. HANNAN, A.M., LL.B., S.T.D., J.C.D.,
Censor Deputatus

Washingtonii, D. C., die 4 aprilis, 1949.

IMPRIMATUR

✠ J. FRANCISCUS A. MCINTYRE, D.D.
Archiepiscopus Angelorum in California

Die 6 aprilis, 1949.

PRINTED IN THE UNITED STATES OF AMERICA
BY
PARKER & COMPANY
LOS ANGELES, CALIF.

TO

MY MOTHER AND FATHER

TABLE OF CONTENTS

Part One

HISTORICAL SYNOPSIS

Part Two

CANONICAL COMMENTARY

INTRODUCTION

"The Catholic priest ought to be distinguished by his detachment. Surrounded by the corruptions of a world in which everything can be bought and sold, he must pass through them utterly free of selfishness. He must holily spurn all vile greed of earthly gains, since he is in search of souls, not of money; of the glory of God, not his own. He is no mercenary working for a temporal recompense, nor yet an employee who, whilst attending conscientiously to duties of his office, at the same time is looking to his career and personal promotion; he is 'the good soldier of Christ' who 'entangleth not himself with secular business; that he please Him to Whom he hath engaged himself.'[1]

"The minister of God is a father of souls; and he knows that his toils and his cares cannot adequately be repaid with wealth and honors of earth. He is not forbidden to receive fitting sustenance, according to the teaching of the Apostle: 'They who serve the altar have their share with the altar. . . . So also the Lord directed that those who preach the gospel should have their living from the gospel.'[2]

"But once called to the 'inheritance of the Lord,' as his very title 'cleric' declares, a priest must expect no other recompense than that promised by Christ to his Apostles: 'Your reward is very great in Heaven.' "[3]

No better introduction to the topic of the present dissertation is available than that offered by the foregoing words of Pius XI in his encyclical on the priesthood.[4]

---

[1]II Tim., II, 3-4.

[2]I Cor., IX, 13-14.

[3]Matt., V, 12.

[4]Litt. encycl. *"Ad Catholici sacerdotii,"* 20 dec. 1935—*Acta Apostolicae Sedis, Commentarium Officiale* (Romae, 1909-) XXVIII (1936), 5, at pp. 28-29 (hereafter cited *AAS*); Vatican Press Translation.

PREFACE

There is an apparent confusion in the decisions of our State and Federal courts relative to the so-called "salary" of Catholic priests and to the moneys received by them as *inter-vivos* offerings for Masses, as offerings for stole fees, and as bequests for Masses.

This confusion about the *nature* of the support of diocesan priests both generally and in particular raises the questions whether, at Canon Law in the United States, a diocesan priest, *qua talis,* receives his support as of the legal nature of "compensation for services rendered," or whether he receives his support from voluntary contributions as of the legal nature of a "gift."

The need for an exposition of the juridical principles, in both Canon Law and the American Common Law, underlying the support of a diocesan priest in the United States, is very urgent.

Recent encroachments by Federal, State, and Municipal Governments upon matters exclusively within the jurisdiction of the Catholic Church, especially in the field of taxation, seem to require such an expression of principles as will correctly represent the true doctrine of the Church that all moneys received by a diocesan priest, *qua talis,* in the United States from Church sources in the exercise of his spiritual functions come to him not of the legal nature of compensation for services rendered but rather of the legal nature of a gift.

The better to enable, on the one hand, secular courts, attorneys, tax officials, legislatures, and others, to appreciate that the financial support accorded to diocesan priests is of the legal nature of a gift, it appears necessary to set forth not only the relation of bishop and priest as created by Canon Law, but also the laws of the Church as to Mass stipends, stole fees, and other offerings, and especially to explore the force in these matters of canon 1529, which to the herein determined extent adopts as Canon Law in the United States the American law on contracts and payments. On the other hand, the better to enable the Catholic hierarchy, the priesthood, the chancery offices, and others, to understand the pertinent provisions of the American secular law as to contracts and payments, including gifts, in their bearing on the support of diocesan priests, it appears necessary to set forth not only the relation of bishop and priest as recognized by the Common Law, but also the constituents of the concept of a "gift" in the Common Law, and to compare this concept in the system of Common Law with the concept in the system of Roman or Civil Law, and in Theology.

The writer takes this occasion to express his gratitude to His Excellency, the Most Rev. John J. Cantwell, D.D., late Archbishop of Los Angeles, and to his successor, His Excellency, the Most Rev. J. Francis A. McIntyre, D.D., for the opportunity of advanced study; to the Faculty of the School of Canon Law of The Catholic University of America; and to his father, Daniel E. O'Brien, A.B., Harvard, LL. B., Harvard, and LL. M., Boston University Graduate School of Law, under whom he has pursued for many years the study of jurisprudence and secular law with special reference to the influence and impact of the Canon Law and the Common Law upon each other; and to his mother, Rena Mannex O'Brien for her constant encouragement in such study.

Chapter I

THE SUPPORT OF PRIESTS IN THE PRIMITIVE CHURCH

In the earliest days of the Church, as the New Testament recounts, the faithful sold all their property, and gave the entire proceeds to the Church.[1] It is not known precisely for how long a time this practice continued.[2] Some historians say that the Christians of Jerusalem continued to give their all to the Church until the destruction of that city.[3] In other congregations in various towns and countries, the Christians kept each their own property, as can be judged from the fact that contributions of money and property were solicited in various places at the instance of St. Paul.[4] All that is certain is that in the first centuries the faithful made generous gifts of the major part of, if not all, their possessions to the Church, which property the Church held in common, and from which the donors as well as the clergy received their support, each according to his need.[5]

As time went on, this early Christian practice of giving all

[1]Acts of the Apostles, II, 44-46; IV, 32-35; V, 1, 4. The primary sources of Canon Law as to the support of priests in the primitive Church are the laws themselves, namely the precepts of the natural and positive divine law, the Apostolic laws, the canons and decrees of the Councils, traditions, and customs. These laws were made by Christ, the Apostles, the Roman Pontiffs, the Councils, and the Bishops. The sources are found in the various documents cited in the footnotes to this dissertation, which was completed in partial fulfillment of the requirements for the doctor's degree in Canon Law, the results of which study were first published by The Catholic University of America Press.

[2]Mourret-Thompson, *History of the Catholic Church* (6 vols., St. Louis: B. Herder Co., 1930-1945), I, 54-55.

[3]Cf. M. Kremer, *Church Support in the United States,* The Catholic University of American Canon Law Studies, n. 61 (Washington, D. C.: The Catholic University of America, 1930), p. 3.

[4]Rom., XV, 26; I Cor., XVI, 1, 2.

[5]Acts of the Apostles, II, 44-46; IV, 32-35; V, 1, 4.

property to the Church gradually disappeared. In its place the Christians began to offer bread, wine, incense, money, the first-fruits of their crops, to God through the Church, after the manner of the Jews. All these free-will gifts to the Church were held in common under the administration of the bishop.[6] From these common funds were supplied all the temporal needs of the Church. The bishop attended to the temporal needs of the priests by dividing these voluntary offerings of the faithful in such a way that the poor, the widows and pilgrims, the clergy and he, himself, received a sufficient support. The priests accordingly lived from these common funds on exactly the same basis as the poor.[7] They were supported by charitable gifts.

Many priests voluntarily gave up their own worldly goods in order to live solely by the altar. St. Prosper of Aquitaine (ca. 390-ca. 463), who is said to be one of the best sources of the history of the early Church,[8] stated that diocesan priests voluntarily lived as paupers in order that they might better serve God and His poor.[9] These priests were supplied by the Church with food and other necessaries of life just as were the poor—from the charitable gifts of the Catholic faithful.[10]

---

[6]Urbanus I (222-230)—Mansi, *Sacrorum Conciliorum Nova et Amplissima Collectio* (53 vols. in 60, Parisiis, 1901-1927), I, 748 (hereafter cited as Mansi); Jaffé, *Regesta Pontificum Romanorum ab condita Ecclesia ad annum post Christum natum MCXCVIII* (2 ed. correctam et auctam auspiciis Gulielmi Wattenbach curaverunt S. Löwenfeld, F. Kaltenbrunner, P. Ewald, 2 tomes in 1 vol., Lipsiae, 1885-1888), n. 87 (Hereafter cited as JK, JE, JL, with number); cf. c. 26, C. XII, q. 1.

[7]*Didache*, c. 13—F. X. Funk, *Patres Apostolici* (2 vols., Tübingen: H. Laupp, 1901), I, 30-32.

[8]Mourret-Thompson, *History of the Catholic Church*, II, p. 603.

[9]C. 9, C. I, q. 2. Cf. The Council of Aix-la-Chapelle, of 816, which considered this custom, whereby priests gave up their worldly goods in order to live solely by the altar so binding that it reiterated Saint Prosper's statements verbatim and declared this to be the binding law of the Frankish Church (c. 108 and c. 111)—*Monumenta Germaniae Historica*, Legum Sectio III, *Concilia*, Tomus II, Pars I, *Concilia Aevi Karolini I*, (ed. A. Werminghoff, Hannoverae et Lipsiae, Bibliopolii Hahman, 1906), pp. 383-384; Mansi, XIV, 215-216.

[10]St. Prosper of Aquitaine, as quoted in the Council of Aix-la-Chapelle (816), c. 107—Mansi, XIV, 214.

In the course of the year 341, the Council of Antioch decreed that the bishop, who had the administration of ecclesiastical property, should see to it that his priests have all that was needed for their suitable support.[11] Supplying support for priests came to be necessary, since practically every priest followed the teaching of St. Prosper by giving up his patrimony and other temporal goods before ordination.[12]

It was necessary for the Church to support its priests, since with the passage of time there developed legislation which forbade the priests to seek their support in secular cares by the labor of their hands or minds. Indeed, the *Canons of the Apostles,* composed in the late fourth or early fifth century, decreed that the clergy who took on such secular occupations were to be deposed.[13]

The same *Canons of the Apostles,* which dealt specifically with the office and duties of a bishop and the qualifications and conduct of the clergy, stated that any priest who was in want was to receive sufficient for his necessities from the common funds of the Church

---

[11]Can. 25: "Episcopus ecclesiasticarum rerum habeat potestatem ad dispensandum erga omnes qui indigent . . . Participet autem et ipse quibus indiget (si tamen indiget) tam in suis quam in fratrum, qui ab eo suscipiuntur, necessariis usibus profuturis, ita ut in nullo qualibet occasione fraudentur, iuxta sanctum Apostolum dicentem: Habentes victum et tegumentum, his contenti simus."—Bruns, *Canones Apostolorum et Conciliorum Saeculorum IV, V, VI, VII* (2 vols., Beroline: Typis et sumptibus G. Reimeri, 1839), I, 87, (hereafter cited as Bruns.).

[12]It appears that any priest who did not in fact renounce his worldly goods and patrimony at the time of his ordination was considered to have forfeited his share of the ecclesiastical distributions ordinarily made for the support of priests. St. Jerome (342-420) is cited by some authors as urging at least a moral obligation, if not a canonical obligation as well, upon all priests, before their ordination to the priesthood, to give away either to their parents or to the poor everything they possessed. St. Jerome is stated to have recommended that no priest be given any support whatsoever from the funds of the Church unless he had so divested himself of all his property before ordination. The passage cited by authors in support of this view has never been located in any extant original writings of St. Jerome. The passage whose authenticity has been both questioned by some and affirmed by others may, however, readily be located in c. 6, C. I, q. 2.

[13]". . . presbiter . . . nequaquam saeculares curas adsumat; sin aliter, deponatur."—*Canones Apostolorum,* c. 7—Mansi, I, 30.

in order that nothing truly necessary for his fitting support be lacking to him.[14]

In the same century, six hundred bishops gathered during the month of October, 451, at Chalcedon for an ecumenical council convoked by the emperor. The representatives of the Pope presided and guided the deliberations. The Council of Chalcedon was chiefly concerned with dogmatic decrees, but promulgated some disciplinary laws. This council restated the mandate of the *Canons of the Apostles* that no bishop, priest, cleric, or monk should engage in any secular traffic or business as a means of financial profit or gain, even as a means of supplying the necessaries for his support.[15] It was obvious to the bishops who attended this council that, if priests were not allowed to engage in secular affairs as a means of support, they would require support from the Church itself. The better to secure the fitting support of the priests, the council decreed that no one could be promoted to the priesthood unless he be specially affiliated with a church which would provide him with his fitting support.[16] The church which provided the priest with support was called in Canon Law his "title,"[17] and no one was to be ordained as a priest unless he had a title of ordination, that is, a church which would provide for his support.

It was a universally understood practice in the Church that the priests were to be provided for throughout their whole life-time. This support was given to the priests whether or not they were actually serving the faithful or the Church itself. Bishop Perpetuus of Tours, in the year 474, offered an interesting example of this. Two of his priests were deposed by him for a cause. They were never again to be permitted to function as priests. Nevertheless Bishop Perpetuus, in following the ecclesiastical tradition re-

---

[14]*Canones Apostolorum,* c. 40: "Ex his [presbiter] autem quae indiget, si tamen indiget, ad suas necessitates . . . percipiat, ut nihil possit eis omnino deesse. Lex enim Dei praecepit ut qui altari servient de altari pascantur, quia nec miles stipendiis propriis arma contra hostes adsumit." —Mansi, I, 38; Bruns, I, 9.

[15]Council of Chalcedon (451), c. 3—Mansi, VII, 374.

[16]Council of Chalcedon (451), c. 6—Mansi, VII, 375.

[17]"Title" is not a univocal word, and has a different technical meaning at the American secular law.

garding the support of priests, ordered that these two men be provided with sufficient support for the remainder of their lives. The support, in their cases, was to come to them by gifts of *sportulae*, or distributions for living expenses, out of the church revenues derived from the voluntary gifts of the faithful.[18]

Pope St. Simplicius (468-483) in the following year, 475, exhibited the same care for the support of priests. Pope St. Simplicius was noted for his efforts to develop the life, both spiritual and temporal, of the Church. He was always concerned to see to it that the diocesan priests were provided with sufficient support from the funds of the Church. In the year 475 he wrote the Bishops Florentius, Equitius, and Severus, instructing them that the portion of ecclesiastical goods set apart for the support of the clergy was to be divided among the priests according to their personal merit.[19]

During this epoch the practice of setting apart a portion of the receipts of the Church for the support of priests was customary throughout the whole Church. Pope St. Gelasius I (492-496), in a letter to the clergy and people of Brindisi, instructed the bishop to divide the revenues of the Church into four portions, one for the fabric or maintenance of the church buildings, one for the poor, one for the bishop, and the fourth to be distributed among the clergy for their support.[20] Though some writers have ascribed the origin of this division of Church funds to Gelasius, still he himself speaks of it as "*dudum rationabiliter . . . decretum,*" having been for some time in force.[21]

The Popes were not content with this single enunciation of the obligation incumbent upon bishops to distribute in a just manner the funds of the Church in such a way as to provide for the suitable

---

[18] L. D'Achery, *Spicilegium sive collectio veterum aliquot scriptorum* (Parisiis, 1723), I, 303.

[19] JK, n. 570; Thiel, *Epistolae Romanorum Pontificum genuinae a S. Hilario (461-468) usque ad S. Hormisdam (514-523)* (Brunsbergae, 1868), pp. 175-176 (hereafter cited as Thiel).

[20] JK, n. 676; Thiel, pp. 380-381. This letter is also found as a general formula used by the Popes in the *Liber Diurnus* as edited by de Rozière (Paris, 1869), n. VI, p. 27.

[21] JK, n. 676; Thiel, p. 378.

support of diocesan priests, but repeated their instructions to this effect again and again in various letters,[22] requiring every bishop on the occasion of his consecration to give a written *cautio* guaranteeing that he would, without diminution, give the priests one-fourth of the receipts of the Church for their support.[23]

In a later portion of his letter to the clergy and people of Brindisi, written in 494, Pope St. Gelasius I (492-496) ordered that the support of priests be distributed to them in accordance with their zeal in fulfilling their religious duties.[24]

The priests were expressly forbidden to take more for their support from the funds of the Church than was permitted them by their bishop,[25] who was ordered to distribute one-quarter of the offerings made by the faithful among the priests for their support. The bishop's own judgment and choice was the sole determinant in deciding the amount of support which each individual priest was to receive in this distribution of the voluntary offerings of the faithful.[26]

The policy enunciated in 475 by Pope St. Simplicius I, and expressed again by Pope St. Gelasius I in 494, that priests should receive an amount of support in accordance with their personal merit and the zeal with which they fulfilled their duties was accepted as the law of the Church and was widespread in its application. The Council of Agde, held in 506, in Languedoc under the presidency of St. Caesarius of Arles (470-542), was attended by twenty-four bishops and ten deputies of absent bishops. Its forty-seven genuine canons dealt with ecclesiastical discipline. This council decreed that priests should be given for their support an amount based upon the merit of the work which they performed for the church to which they were attached.[27]

---

[22]E.g., JK, nn. 647, 675, 676.

[23]*Liber Diurnus,* n. LXXIV, p. 149.

[24]Gelasius, *Ep. xv*—Thiel, p. 380.

[25]Gelasius, *Ep. xiv*—Thiel, p. 378; JK, n. 636.

[26]JK, n. 740; Thiel, p. 498.

[27]Council of Agde, c. 36: "Clerici omnes, qui ecclesiae fideliter vigilanter deserviunt, stipendia sanctis laboribus debita secundum servitii sui meritum vel ordinationem canonum a sacerdotibus consequantur."—Mansi, VIII, 331; Bruns, II, 153.

Five years later, in the year 511, the I Council of Orleans was convoked by King Clovis (481-511). Thirty-three bishops assisted and passed thirty-one decrees. Clovis recognized and accepted as valid and binding in his kingdom the decrees of this council, which thus appear as the first written *modus vivendi* between the Frankish State and the Church. This council ordered that the ancient canons should be observed with reference to the bishop's control over church property, and also with reference to his obligation of distributing adequate support to the priests of his territory.[28]

In the first part of the sixth century, the bishop exercised extensive administrative powers in each detail of the functioning of his diocese and of the various churches therein. However, the increasing number of rural churches made it a practical necessity for the bishop to entrust the temporal welfare of the churches to resident priests. Parochial property thus began to acquire a stability theretofore unknown. All revenue, save a portion for the support of the bishop himself, was left with the local church for the upkeep of the buildings and the support of the priests attached thereto.[29]

When members of the cathedral clergy were assigned to another church, the bishop sometimes permitted them to continue to receive for their support the same portion of the fruits which they had been accustomed to receive while in the service of the cathedral. The III National Council of Orleans, held in May of 538, was attended by nineteen bishops,[30] who discussed this practice of permitting members of the cathedral clergy to receive double support at the same time, once from the former appointment at the cathedral, and once from their new appointment. The council recommended that such priests be supported only by their new titles, although it left the matter to the prudence of their individual bishop.[31] In addition to recommending that diocesan priests be

[28]I Council of Orleans (511), c. 5—Bruns, II, 162.

[29]Council of Carpentras (527)—Bruns, II, 175; cf. II Council of Braga (572), c. 2—Mansi, IX, 839.

[30]Landon, *A Manual of Councils of the Holy Catholic Church*, new and rev. ed., (2 vols., Edinburgh: John Grant, reprint in 1909), II, 7.

[31]III Council of Orleans (538), c. 18—Bruns, II, 197-198.

supported by only one church at one time, the same council enacted into law that each local church bear the burden of providing adequate support for the priests attached thereto.[32]

St. Isidore of Seville (560-636), said by some to be the most learned bishop of his age, in a letter to Bishop Leudefrede, stated that the law of the Church at that time required the diocesan econome[33] to "dispense the contributions made for the support of the clergy, the poor, and the widows." In all this work the econome was subject to the supervision of the bishop, in whom was vested the responsibility of seeing to it that every priest received adequate support.[34]

Pope St. Gregory I (590-604), one of the most notable figures in ecclesiastical history, was vigilant in watching lest the property of the Church be in any way misappropriated. He found time to write instructions on even minute details, and was said to have left no complaint unattended to, even from the humblest of the diocesan priests. Although he was inflexible with regard to the proper application of church revenues, insisting that others should be as strict as he was in the administration of these funds, and watched carefully lest any of the priests take too much for his support, he was equally insistent that the priests receive a sufficiency for their adequate support. In a letter to Leo, Bishop of Carthage, written in the year 598, Pope St. Gregory called attention to the obligation incumbent upon every bishop to divide without diminution one

---

[32] III Council of Orleans (538), c. 5—Bruns, II, 193.

[33] The diocesan econome was, since the time of the Council of Chalcedon (451), appointed for the actual financial administration under the supervision of the bishop. Spanish conciliar law (Council of Seville in 619, c. 9 —Mansi, X, 560) decreed that bishops appoint economes for the administration of diocesan property in order to prevent any suspicion of episcopal maladministration. (Cf. J. Comyns, *Papal and Episcopal Administration of Church Property,* The Catholic University of America Canon Law Studies, n. 147 (Washington, D. C.: The Catholic University of America Press, 1942), p. 33, (hereafter cited as *Administration*).

[34] *Ep. ad Leudefredum,* n. 15—Migne, *Patrologiae Cursus Completus, Series Latina* (221 vols., Parisiis, 1844-1864), LXXXIII, 897 (hereafter cited as *MPL*).

entire quarter of the church's receipts among the priests, deacons, and clergy, in a discreet manner, for their support.[35]

The detailed manner of the division and the amount of support to be received by each priest was left by Gregory to the discretion of the bishop. The bishop, however, although he could determine the exact amount of support to be received by a priest, was nevertheless, under other ecclesiastical legislation, required to see to it that each priest had all that was truly necessary for his adequate support and that none of his priests was in need.[36]

Of considerable interest in the United States, which derives its secular law from the English Common Law, is a response sent by Pope St. Gregory I (590-604) in the year 601 to St. Augustine, Bishop of England. Although there is some question as to the authenticity of the response, nevertheless it is considered by many scholars of authority to have been authentic, particularly since its content, as regards the support of priests, was in complete accord with the ancient custom of the Church. The Pope emphasized the ecclesiastical law regarding the support of priests with a statement that it had long been the custom of the Apostolic See to order all bishops to divide the receipts of the church into four portions, one of which was to be used by the bishop for his household, a second to be used in repairing the church buildings and maintaining divine worship, a third to be given to the poor, and the fourth to be given to the clergy for their support.[37]

Under Pope St. Gregory I it was customary for all priests, whether they were serving in the then equivalent of our present day diocesan assignments, or whether they were not actively engaged in the care of the souls of the faithful, to receive a portion of the revenues of the church for their support.[38] Priests who

---

[35]*Epistolarum Liber 7*, n. 8—Mansi, I, 90.

[36]Council of Antioch (341), c. 25—Bruns, I, 87; c. 23, C. XII, q. 1.

[37]"Mos est apostolicae sedis ordinatis episcopis praeceptum tradere, ut de omni stipendio, quod accidit, quattuor fieri debeant portiones, una videlicet episcopo et familiae eius propter hospitalitatem et susceptionem, alio clero, tertia vero pauperibus, quarta ecclesiis reparandis."—JE, n. 1843; Mansi, X, 415.

[38]JE, n. 1112; cf. JE, n. 1086.

were ill were provided for in a similar way, as is evidenced by a command from Pope St. Gregory to a Bishop Candidus to give an ailing priest the "usual" sum.[39]

The legislation of the primitive Church shows that the priests were supported by the Church from the offerings of the faithful. There was a voluntary transfer of money or of property from the faithful, both as individuals and as state officials making grants from the government,[40] for the support of the priests. Nowhere in the ecclesiastical legislation is there any indication that there was any legal consideration involved. Instead it appears to have been the ancient custom in the primitive Church, as said St. Prosper of Aquitaine, that the priests voluntarily lived as paupers in order that they might the better serve God and His poor, and that the priests were supplied by the Church with food and other necessities of life, just as were the poor, by means of voluntary charitable gifts.[41]

---

[39]JE, n. 1161; Mansi, IX, 1086-1087.

[40]As, for example, gifts from Emperors such as Constantine.

[41]C. 9, C. I, q. 2; cf. *supra*, p. 2.

Chapter II

THE SUPPORT OF PRIESTS IN THE UNITED STATES IS OF THE SAME NATURE AS THE SUPPORT OF PRIESTS IN THE PRIMITIVE CHURCH

The earliest ecclesiastical legislation in the United States regarding the support of diocesan priests was enacted in the year 1791. In that year there was held a synod at which it was decreed that the priests in the United States be supported in accordance with the ancient custom of the Church[1] by means of the voluntary offerings of the faithful, which were to be divided into three parts, one of which was to be applied for the maintenance or fabric of the church, a second for the poor, and a third for the support of the priests.

The Synod of 1791 was traditionally accurate when it stated that the support of priests in the United States was to be after the manner of the primitive Church. It deliberately by-passed European ecclesiastical legislation and customs regarding the manner of support of diocesan priests. The introduction herein of any other material concerning the support of priests *in Europe* from the seventh century to the *Decretum* of Gratian, or from Gratian to the Council of Trent, or from the Council of Trent to the Code of Canon Law, might tend to confuse the legal problems involved in this study. It is accordingly omitted as irrelevant.

The synodal legislation of 1791 is, in the opinion of Guilday (1884-1947),[2] the cornerstone of the edifice erected by our prelates

---

[1]1791 Synod, Statutes V, VI, VII. Note Statute VII: "Oblationes iuxta *antiquum Ecclesiae morem* [italics inserted] dividantur . . . ita ut una Sacerdotis sustentationi . . . applicetur."—*Acta et Decreta Sacrorum Conciliorum Recentiorum, Collectio Lacensis* (7 vols., Friburgi Brisgoviae: Herder, 1870-1892), III, 3 (hereafter cited *Coll. Lac.*).

[2]P. Guilday, *A History of the Councils of Baltimore, 1791-1884* (New York: The Macmillan Company, 1932), p. 63 (hereafter cited as *History*).

during the century which followed. The Statutes of the Synod of 1791 were considered as the *Magna Carta* for all subsequent American ecclesiastical legislation in the Baltimore Councils, both Provincial and Plenary.[3]

In the Synod of 1791 it was decreed that the people be admonished of the offerings made by primitive Christians at the time of Mass, and it was further decreed that in every congregation persons be appointed to collect the offerings of the faithful. These offerings were, according to the ancient practice of the Church, to be divided into three parts, so that one was to be applied to the sustenance and support of the priests, another to the relief of the poor, and the third to the procuring of all things requisite for divine service and the fabric or maintenance of the church.[4] If, however, there was in existence any other provision whereby the priest received his support, then that portion of the offerings otherwise for the sustenance of the priest was ordered applied to the fabric or maintenance of the church.[5]

The Synod of 1791 felt it needful to legislate that the faithful be warned that those who did not contribute to the support of the priests were violating the Divine Law and would be answerable to God.[6] The Synod even went so far as to indicate that those who failed to contribute to the support of the priests were to be held unworthy of absolution for depriving the poor of opportunities spiritual and temporal.[7]

---

[3]Guilday, *History,* p. 62.

[4]1791 Synod, Statutes V, VI, VII—*Coll. Lac.,* III, 3.

[5]1791 Synod, Statute VII—*Coll. Lac.,* III, 3.

[6]1791 Synod, Statute XXIII—*Coll. Lac.,* III, 6.

[7]In 1816 the Sacred Congregation for the Propagation of the Faith replied to a question proposed by the Bishop of Bardstown (Louisville) that the faithful are obliged to provide support for the church, but added that the offerings should be voluntary and that the sacrament of baptism was not to be refused to anyone in the families of those who failed to support the priests. *Collectanea S. C. de Propaganda Fide* (2 vols., Romae, 1907), n. 713 (hereafter cited as *Collectanea); Codicis Iuris Canonici Fontes* (9 vols., Romae: 1923-1939), n. 4705 (hereafter cited as *Fontes* with number). The III Plenary Council of Baltimore (1884) forbade the refusal of absolution to any one found wanting in this respect, and the reason was added, namely, that there exists no moral certainty as to the gravity of the

In the Synod of 1791, the faithful were notified that there would be issued a Pastoral Letter with additional regulations regarding the support of the diocesan priests.[8] In the following year, less than six months after the formal promulgation of the decrees of the Synod, Bishop Carroll (+1815) issued the Pastoral Letter which had been promised. In this Pastoral Letter he stated that it would be of little use to prepare priests for the work of the ministry if afterwards they would not have sufficient and necessary support.

Previously, in the colonial days, there were funds adequate for their subsistence and made available from the estates of the Society of Jesus. These, however, had been renounced in behalf of diocesan priests, shortly after Bishop Carroll had been consecrated.[9] By 1792 it became "absolutely necessary to resort to the means of supporting public worship and instruction which are prescribed not only by natural equity, but likewise by the positive ordinances of divine wisdom." [10] It was in obedience to this divine ordinance that primitive Christians presented their offerings on the altar of the Lord, signifying by this act that they were intended not so much for their pastors, as that they were consecrated to God Himself.[11]

The Church, said Bishop Carroll in his Pastoral Letter, regarded the offerings of the faithful as consecrated to God Himself, and decreed in its canons that the religious oblations should be utilized first for the maintenance of the ministers of the sanctuary,

---

obligation.—*Acta et Decreta Concilii Plenarii Baltimorensis Tertii, A.D. MDCCCLXXXIV* (Baltimorae: Murphy & Co., 1886), n. 272 (hereafter cited as III Plenary Council of Baltimore, with number of decree). Cf. *The Jurist* (Washington, D. C., 1941-) I (1941), 343.

8 1791 Synod, Statute XXIII—*Coll. Lac.*, III, 6.

9 T. Hughes, *History of the Society of Jesus in North America: Colonial and Federal* (4 vols., Text: 2 vols., Documents: 2 vols., New York: Longmans Green & Co., 1907-1917) (hereafter cited as Hughes, *Text*, or Hughes, *Documents*, with number, section, and page of volume), *Documents*, I, I, 411, and I, II, 699.

10 P. Guilday (Editor) *National Pastorals of the American Hierarchy* (Washington, D.C.: N.C.W.C., 1923), p. 7 (hereafter cited as *National Pastorals)*.

11 C. 26, C. XII, q. 1.

and with this need properly satisfied the remainder should be applied towards the relief of the poor, for the building and repairing of churches and places of worship necessary for public convenience, and for the decent ordering of divine worship.

Each Catholic was, by the Synod of 1791 and the Pastoral Letter of 1792, reminded of the moral obligation of bearing his proportion of the common and necessary expenses for the support of public worship—an obligation which had not been insisted on previously so long as the assistance of the faithful was unnecessary for the support of the priests, which support had up to that time been provided from the estates operated by the Jesuit fathers. To render more certain the support of the diocesan priests in the United States, Bishop Carroll ordered that they require at marriages, burials, and funeral services, a certain "very moderate compensation," [12] which they were at the same time forbidden to require from those who, on account of their poverty, would be overburdened by any payment of such "compensation." [13]

By 1837, when the III Provincial Council of Baltimore was held, the support of priests was still so inadequate that the second decree ordered that the faithful be admonished of the duty incumbent upon them to provide a decent support for the diocesan priests both in sickness and in health.[14] In addition, a Pastoral Letter was issued in connection with this council. In this letter the bishops emphasized to the laity their moral obligation to provide for the support of the priests by their voluntary contributions.[15] In many instances, to be sure, some Catholics exerted themselves in a manner very creditable to themselves and beneficial to religion by contributing without any clerical urging to the support of their priests. The laity were reminded, however, that almost all of the churches in the United States were built chiefly by the laborious exertions of

---

[12]"Compensation" is not a univocal term. As used by Bishop Carroll it has a different meaning from its use in American Law to denote a binding contractual obligation at law resulting from services rendered. Cf. *infra*, pp. 48 *ff*.

[13]*National Pastorals*, p. 12.

[14]*Coll. Lac.*, III, 56.

[15]*National Pastorals*, pp. 110-111.

the priests, that the whole income[16] of these churches was produced by the activities of the priest, and that, if the priest were to cease to officiate, the revenue of the church would be small indeed.

In this same Pastoral Letter of April 22, 1837, the bishops advised the faithful that the priests were prohibited by the canons of the Church from engaging in business or in any other work for financial gain, and that the priests must be wholly occupied with their religious duties.[17] Since the priest could not provide his own support, the congregation was expected to support him.[18] The amount which priests received for their support at that time was comparatively moderate, sometimes wretchedly small. Priests were pressed, moreover, by solicitations for aid from the distressed laity, and by demands for the advancement of religion in a missionary country, which resulted in depriving them of the opportunity, even if they had the inclination, of laying up for themselves any provision for old age or infirmity.[19]

In 1840 the bishops assembled for the IV Provincial Council of Baltimore, wherein they discussed the support of diocesan priests and enacted legislation. In this legislation it is clear that the priests were not considered to be serving as employees of their congregation, or as being engaged in any pursuit for monetary or personal gain:

> "Let the priests care for the congregation committed to them, not forced, but spontaneously, according to God; not for the sake of any base gain but voluntarily . . . in order that . . . they may obtain an imperishable crown of glory" (from Christ the Prince of Pastors).[20]

On May 9, 1852, the bishops of the entire United States assembled with the six archbishops in the Cathedral at Baltimore for the

---

[16]"Income" is not a univocal term. As used by the bishops in their Pastoral Letter it did not have the normal technical sense as found in American Secular Law. Cf. *infra*, pp. 115 *ff*.

[17]*National Pastorals*, p. 111.

[18]III Provincial Council of Baltimore (1837), Decree 2—*Coll. Lac.*, III, 56.

[19]*National Pastorals*, p. 111.

[20]Decree 10—*Coll. Lac.*, III, 71. (Translation by the writer.).

I Plenary Council. The twenty-five decrees which they enacted may be viewed substantially as a re-affirmation of the legislation which had been passed in all the Provincial assemblies up to that year. Regarding the support of priests, the I Plenary Council restated the decrees passed in the Provincial Councils.[21]

Diocesan synods and provincial councils began to be held in numbers in other parts of the country. Little was done, however, with respect to the support of diocesan priests in these synods and councils other than to restate or implement the previously enacted Baltimore decrees.[22]

Fourteen years later, in 1866, the archbishops and bishops of the entire United States assembled for the II Plenary Council. Like the preceding council of national scope, it was held in Baltimore. The support of the priests was an item of no small importance, and once again the legislation of all the previous provincial councils and of the I Plenary Council on that subject was confirmed and again promulgated.[23]

The faithful were again urged to make voluntary contributions for the support of their priests. The decision as to just how much support each individual priest should receive was left to the decision of his bishop. It was decreed that if a bishop decided that a priest had sufficient support, that priest could not leave the station to which he was assigned.[24]

A priest was to be supported even when through his own fault he had become unworthy of filling an ecclesiastical office or assignment with the care of souls. The Sacred Congregation for the Propagation of the Faith, in a response to the Bishop of Natchez, on February 4, 1873, emphatically declared that a priest cannot be deprived of his means of support, unless, after repeated warnings, he refuses to amend, and demonstrates his contumacy. It was stated therein that grave offenses committed by a priest, such as may even justify his deposition from office, did not warrant the bishop

[21]Decree 2—*Coll. Lac.*, III, 145.

[22]Guilday, *History*, p. 174.

[23]II Plenary Council of Baltimore, Decree 108—*Coll. Lac.*, III, 431.

[24]II Plenary Council of Baltimore, Decree 108, re-enacting verbatim Decree 1 of the I Provincial Council of Baltimore—*Coll. Lac.*, III, 25.

in refusing him support. The Church, like a compassionate mother, was to supply him his daily bread and to endeavor to bring about an amendment from his evil course.[25]

By 1884 the support of the diocesan priests in the United States had gradually begun to be less of an economic problem. Still, when in November of that year the archbishops and bishops assembled in Baltimore for the III Plenary Council, they took up the subject and once again legislated on the support of the priests. It was decreed that the bishop should establish a fund from which subsidies were to be given for the decent support of any priests who were unable to take care of souls in churches and accordingly received no support from a congregation. This inability to function normally as a diocesan priest attached to a mission was generally due to illness, although other causes could intervene. In its care for the sick priests and their support, the III Plenary Council of Baltimore was but implementing previous legislation.[26] For the priest who was able to perform his ministerial duties the III Plenary Council of Baltimore enacted legislation that provided for his fitting and adequate support.[27]

In order to prevent any suspicion that the priests were seeking money for their personal gain, bishops were ordered to select a fixed and definite sum which the priests could take from the funds of their respective churches for their support. This sum was given the name of *congrua* in imitation of the ancient terminology of the Church. As a synonymous definition to explain the matter, so that the laity could understand what was meant by *congrua,* the council added a form of the Latin word *"salarium,"* often translated in English as "salary." [28] The word "salary," as used officially in this and all subsequent Catholic Church legislation in the United States in respect to the support of priests, was clearly identified with the

---

[25]*Collectanea,* n. 1394.

[26]III Plenary Council of Baltimore, Decree 71; cf. II Plenary Council of Baltimore, Decree 90—*Coll. Lac.,* III, 56; cf. III Provincial Council of Baltimore, Decree 2—*Coll. Lac.,* III, 428.

[27]Decree 273.

[28]III Plenary Council of Baltimore, Decree 273: "congruae seu salarii nomine percipi possit."

term *congrua,* the meaning of which had become crystalized by centuries of usage in the Church.[29]

Priests were warned, moreover, to be content with receiving less for their support than the amount selected by the bishop and fixed for their *congrua* or salary if their mission or missions were unable to supply that amount from the voluntary contributions of the faithful.[30]

---

[29]"Salary" is not a univocal word. The money paid to a diocesan priest from parish or diocesan funds for his sustentation is often called his "salary," and frequently is confused with the American Common Law term "salary," which requires a Common Law contract of employment. When used in its strict canonical sense to designate one of the means of support for a diocesan priest in the United States it is not used in exactly the same sense as when used in the secular system of Common Law. It is submitted that many of the difficulties in understanding just what is the nature of the support yielding to diocesan priests in the United States tend to disappear when it is realized that "salary" is not a univocal term, and actually has several different meanings.

At the time the III Plenary Council of Baltimore employed the word "salarium", the secular cases involving controversies over support between priests and bishops had unanimously declared that no contract of employment existed between a bishop and a priest and consequently the money which a priest received for his support did not constitute a "salary" as that term is understood in the secular law. "Salarium", as used by the III Plenary Council meant a voluntary contribution, a gift. The III Plenary Council had a right to rely on the principles enunciated in the secular cases to the effect that State courts would not construe the support-money received by priests as compensation under a contract of employment.

Rose v. Vertin, 46 Mich. 457, (1881);

Tuigg v. Sheehan, 101 Pa. 363, (1882).

[30]"Lest the right order of justice be disturbed, and the suspicion of base greed injure the reputation of the priests, we decree that the bishops . . . shall set a fixed and definite sum which shall be received by the rectors of churches under the name of *congrua* or salary. The priests, however, shall be content with a smaller amount in case their mission or missions be unable to supply from its annual receipts this sum . . ." "Ne tamen rectus justitiae ordo turbetur, nec integram suspicio lucri minuat famam, decernimus ut Episcopi pro singulis suis dioecesibus in synodo, vel extra synodum e consultorum consilio, fixam ratamque definiant summam quae ab ecclesiarum rectoribus congruae seu salarii nomine percipi possit. Minori tamen summa contenti sint oportet sacerdotes casu quo eorum missio vel missiones per reditus suos annuos statutam congruam suppeditare nequeant, cujus rei

Furthermore, it was decreed that neither the bishop personally, nor the diocese, was under any obligation in Canon Law to supply any defect in the amount of the *congrua* or salary received by a priest for his support in case his mission or missions were unable to supply the amount fixed by the bishop. It was required, however, as a minimum, that every priest be provided sufficient support for his food and shelter.[31]

Priests were cautioned to take from the church funds this money for their support within the period of one year from the time it fell due. If they did not take their support money, *congrua* or sal-

---

judex erit Ordinarius, audito consultorum consilio."—III Plenary Council of Baltimore, Decree n. 273. (Translation by the writer.).

[31]"We are unwilling that the salary be taken from the funds of the churches which have already been acquired; and the bishop or the diocese is bound by no law to supply any deficiency in salary if the missionary priests for any cause receive no salary or even receive a smaller amount, provided . . . they are not lacking in the necessary food and shelter . . ." "Nolumus enim ut salaria ex bonis ecclesiae jam acquisitis percipiantur; et Episcopus vel dioecesis nulla lege tenetur salarii defectum supplere, si qua de causa sacerdotes missionarii nullum vel justum minus acceperint, dummodo tamen, juxta dictum Apostoli (I Tim., 6, 8) necessaria ad alimenta et tegumenta non desint, nisi forte hic ipse necessariorum defectus, iudicio Episcopi cum suis consultoribus, gravi culpa ipsius missionarii accidisset." —III Plenary Council of Baltimore, Decree n. 273. (Translation by the writer.).

In the years immediately preceding the III Plenary Council of Baltimore (1884), priests, in two cases, had sued their *bishops* for "salary-support" in the secular courts, resulting in decisions adverse to them in the State courts of last resort.

In one case, *Rose v. Vertin*, 46 Mich. 457, (1881), the claim was for two years' "salary" for services actually rendered a congregation by the priest, the theory of the priest's claim being that, on default by the congregation, the bishop was *personally* liable in an action of contract (of employment).

In the other case, *Tuigg v. Sheehan*, 101 Pa. 363, (1882), the priest sued his bishop for "salary-support" for a period of years during which the bishop had refused to assign him to diocesan service from which he would have received support. The theory of this suit was not on a contract express or implied in fact but was based on the duty of the Church to provide its priests with support.

The relevant legislation of the III Plenary Council set forth in notes 31 and 32 may well have been prompted by the mischief of these two cases in the secular courts.

ary so-called, within the year, it was conclusively presumed that they did not need this sum, or any part thereof, for their support, and had given it back to the church.[32]

This legislation of the III Plenary Council of Baltimore continues in force as something outside the Code of Canon Law, which does not explicitly provide any formula for fixing the amount of support to be received by diocesan priests in the United States.[33]

The obligation which rests upon the Church to provide support for its diocesan priests became crystalized in the provision of the Code of Canon Law which states that the bishop must provide each priest whom he ordains on the title of service of the diocese with a benefice, or an office, or a subsidy sufficient for his adequate support.[34]

---

[32]". . . We order priests not to neglect to take their *congrua* or salary, unless they wish to give it to the church, at an opportune time . . . we declare that those who fail to take the money due them on that account within one year, or at least do not demand it in writing from the Ordinary . . . by that very fact have renounced their right, and on no account may ever in the future demand such sum . . ." ". . . Ob gravia secus oritura incommoda monemus sacerdotes ut congruam suam seu salarium, nisi id ecclesiae donare velint, opportune tempore exigere et percipere non negligant. Ideo statuimus ut eos qui pecuniam ea ratione sibi debitam infra annum a termino quo solvenda erat, percipere omiserint, aut saltem non exegerint per scriptum ab Ordinario vel ejus cancellario probatum, eo ipso renuntiasse juri suo, eosque nullo titulo postea summam istam repetere posse."—III Plenary Council of Baltimore, Decree n. 281. (Translation by the writer.).

[33]J. Barrett, *A Comparative Study of the Third Plenary Council of Baltimore and the Code,* The Catholic University of America Canon Law Studies, n. 83 (Washington, D. C.: The Catholic University of America, 1932), p. 101 (hereafter cited as *Comparative Study).*

[34]*Codex Iuris Canonici Pii X Pontificis Maximi iussu digestus, Benedicti Papae XV auctoritate promulgatus* (Romae: Typis Polyglottis Vaticanis, 1917), Canon 981 (hereafter simply cited with the number of the Canon).

CHAPTER III

THE SUPPORT OF DIOCESAN PRIESTS UNDER THE CODE OF CANON LAW—PRELIMINARY CONCEPTS

ARTICLE 1. INTRODUCTORY CONCEPTS

The support of diocesan priests from ecclesiastical sources in the United States at the present day, apart from food and shelter, is generally effected by delivery to them of cash or bank checks. Every such delivery and acceptance has legal effects and a legal cause.

Two separate and distinct systems of law, each with its own concepts and terminology, need to be considered with respect to the nature of support of diocesan priests in the United States—Canon Law and the American Law prevailing in the place where the priest receives his support.[1] This follows since some aspects of the support of diocesan priests in the United States are temporal matters annexed to a spiritual matter. Passing of legal title to the temporal money, or its equivalent, received by priests depends upon the civil law of the place where the transfer is made. The Church legislates to this effect in canon 1529, by providing that the law of the place on contracts and payments of all kinds, as to their temporal aspects, is to be recognized and adopted as part of Canon Law, with the same effects of licitness, validity, enforceability, unless the state law contravenes the Divine Law or the matter is otherwise duly provided for by Canon Law.[2]

[1]The support of diocesan priests is herein restricted to its legal aspects exclusively. No consideration is herein given to any obligation in conscience or under moral theology as to the support of diocesan priests. Cf. R. Pound, "A Comparison of the Ideals of Law," *Harvard Law Review* (Cambridge, Massachusetts: Harvard Law Review Publishing Association, 1887-   ), XLVII (1933), 11 (hereafter cited as *HLR*).

[2]Canon 1529—Quae ius civile in territorio statuit de contractibus tam in genere, quam in specie, sive nominatis sive innominatis, et de solutionibus, eadem iure canonico in materia ecclesiastica iisdem cum effectibus serventur, nisi iuri divino contraria sint aut aliud iure canonico caveatur.

The law of the state as to the passing of legal title is, as it were, canonized and made ecclesiastical law as much as the provisions contained explicitly in the Code of Canon Law itself.[3] The secular law of the place is thus recognized, given effect, and applied by the Code of Canon Law—*as Canon Law*![4] This is a new and important declaration of the law of the Church. Previous to the effective date of the Code of Canon Law, the Church adopted Roman Law in respect to certain contracts and payments. By the Code of Canon Law the Roman Law was dismissed and abandoned by the Church on this point.[5] In lieu of Roman Law the law of the place was adopted as to contracts and payments. This recognition and application by the Code of Canon Law of the law of the place suppresses pre-Code treatments of the subject and sanctions a new general principle.[6]

Because of the application of two systems of law and of the mutual recognition and adoption of some of their principles, procedures, and adjudications, much misunderstanding has arisen between representatives of Canon Law and representatives of American Law. This misunderstanding is due, in large part, to a lack of adequate communication on both sides. In designation of the support of diocesan priests, words have been used interchangeably in the two systems of law, words not univocal, but rather possessing one technical meaning in Canon Law in general and a

---

[3]E. Heston, *The Alienation of Church Property in the United States,* The Catholic University of America Canon Law Studies, n. 132 (Washington, D. C.: The Catholic University of America Press, 1941), p. 66 (hereafter cited *Alienation*).

[4]G. Vromant, *De Bonis Ecclesiae Temporalibus,* Museum Lessianum—Section Théologique, n. 19 (Louvain: Museum Lessianum, 1927), pp. 289-291 (hereafter cited as *De Bonis Ecclesiae);* cf. P. Gasparri, *Schema Codicis Iuris Canonici* (Romae: Typis Polyglottis Vaticanis, 1913), p. 351 (hereafter cited as *Schema Codicis).*

[5]F. Wernz—P. Vidal, *Ius Canonicum ad Codicis Normam Exactum* (7 vols. in 8, Romae: apud Aedes Universitatis Gregorianae, 1923-), IV, II, 331 (hereafter cited as *Ius Canonicum).*

[6]Wernz-Vidal, *Ius Canonicum,* IV, I, 331; A. Vermeersch—J. Creusen, *Epitome Iuris Canonici* (3 vols., Vols. I and II, 2 ed. 1923-1925; Vol. III, 6 ed., 1946, Mechliniae-Romae: Dessain), II, 485 (hereafter cited as *Epitome).*

different technical meaning in American Law, and after the effective date of canon 1529 with two different technical meanings at Canon Law in the United States.[7] The suggestion of Mr. Justice Holmes (1841-1935),[8]

> "a word is not a crystal, transparent and unchanged; it is the skin of a living thought and may vary greatly in color and content according to the circumstances and the time in which it is used,"

is particularly applicable in a situation like the present where two different systems of law are in juxtaposition, each with an impact upon the other.

Representatives of the American Law should keep in mind that the juristic principles and procedure of the Canon Law system which may appear at first sight untenable to them are often older than those which they have been accustomed to think of as having existed from time immemorial, older in fact than the *Magna Carta* of King John (1199-1216), and that millions of Catholics have been governed by them from the time of the formation of the Christian Church and are still governed by them without any question about their entire propriety.[9]

Representatives of the Canon Law must not forget that many of the jural postulates of the American Secular Laws are predicated on Divine Positive Law and are identical with the principles of justice and charity advocated by the Fathers of the Church. That in the course of time and amid changing circumstances there should be a variance in the positive law of these two systems which have such different ends was inevitable.[10]

---

[7]The word "salary" is one such word with a technical meaning at Canon Law in general, a different technical meaning at American Law, both technical meanings at Canon Law in the United States, plus an additional technical meaning flowing from its use in the III Plenary Council of Baltimore. Cf. *supra*, p. 17.

[8]*Towne v. Eisner,* 245 U.S. 418 (1918).

[9]Pound, in *Bonacum v. Harrington,* 65 Neb. 831 (1902).

[10]Cf. A. Blat, *Commentarium Textus Codicis Iuris Canonici* (6 vols., Romae: Libreria del Collegio "Angelico", 1919-1927), IV, 546 (hereafter cited as *Commentarium).*

Since the present misunderstanding has arisen to a large degree because of the use in the two systems of law of the same words which are not univocal, many of the difficulties in understanding the nature of support of diocesan priests in the United States will tend to disappear with the realization that some of the words involved, although perhaps spelled and pronounced identically by Canon Law and American Law scholars, are nevertheless of different technical connotation in each system of law, and even in the same system may have different technical meanings so that divergent legal consequences may flow therefrom.[11]

Although the fundamental current law of the Church is that the law of the place as to contracts and payments is recognized, given effect, and applied by the Code of Canon Law *as Canon Law,*[12] nevertheless the Church has placed two limitations upon its adoption of the law of the place as Canon Law. If the law of the place be contrary to the Divine Law, then Canon Law repudiates such civil law and does not adopt it. If the law of the place be contrary to an express provision of Canon Law, whether general or particular in a given territory, then such civil law is not recognized, given effect, or applied as Canon Law.[13]

Standard Canon Law commentators have listed the various canons of the Code which, in their opinion, may or do exclude the adoption of the law of the place as Canon Law.[14] It is submitted

[11]Cf. Blat, *Commentarium* IV, 546. "A sale is a sale at Amsterdam and at New York. Yet the legal understanding and treatment of the transaction in the two places may be very different."—R. Pound, "A Comparison of the Ideals of Law," *HLR,* XLVII (1933), 1, at p. 11.

[12]Vromant, *De Bonis Ecclesiae,* p. 291; cf. Gasparri, *Schema Codicis,* p. 351, c. 809.

[13]G. Cocchi, *Commentarium in Codicem Iuris Canonici* (5 vols. in 8, 4. ed., Taurinorum Augustae: Marietti, 1930-1938), VI, 410-411 (hereafter cited as *Commentarium);* C. Berutti, *Institutiones Iuris Canonici* (6 vols. in 7 [Vol. II, Pars II, et Vol. V nondum edita] Taurini: Marietti, 1936-) IV, 509 (hereafter cited as *Institutiones);* Blat, *Commentarium,* IV, 545-546; Vermeersch-Creusen, *Epitome,* II, 485; Wernz-Vidal, *Ius Canonicum,* IV, II, 331-332.

[14]E.g. Canons 122; 536; 569; 579-582; 614; 1479; 1495, §2; 1513-1517; 1531; 1532; 1535-1537; 1540; 1542; 1543; 1545-1551. It is to be noted that none of these canons cited by the various canon law commentators applies to the nature of support of diocesan priests. The recommendation of

however that, to determine whether the two exceptions to canon 1529 are present and applicable as to the nature of support of diocesan priests in the United States, it is necessary to set forth *both* the Canon Law and the American Law on the subject, and then by examination to ascertain whether the American Law is *de facto* either contrary to the Divine Law or contrary to any express provision of Canon Law.[15]

In either of these instances the Canon Law must prevail and the American Law on contracts and payments will not be recognized, given effect, and applied as Canon Law.[16] If, however, it appears that the American Law as to those aspects of contracts and payments over which the state has jurisdiction is contrary neither to the Divine Law nor to Canon Law, then the American Law on contracts and payments is *the Canon Law* itself as to the nature of support of diocesan priests in the United States.[17] The determina-

---

Wernz-Vidal *(Ius Canonicum,* IV, II, 332) that the civil law commentators be consulted in each case seems to be a more legal approach than the mere accepting of the extrinsic authority of the various canon law commentators who give their own opinions as to which laws are, or may be, contrary to the provisions of Canon Law. Cocchi *(Commentarium,* VI, 410-411) also recommends consultation of the civil law authors in each case; Blat *(Commentarium,* IV, 546) likewise recommends such consultation of the civil law authors *qua* Canon Law commentators under the provisions of Canon 1529.

[15]Blat, *Commentarium,* IV, 546: ". . . *aut aliud* ac 'ius civile statuit' diversum vel oppositum vel ultra illud *iure canonico caveatur*"; Cocchi, *Commentarium,* VI, 411: ". . . nisi praescriptum civile contrarium sit . . . *expressae legi canonicae* sive generali, sive particulari"; Vermeersch-Creusen, *Epitome,* II, 485; "quotiescunque dispositio canonica generalis vel particularis cum iure civili componi nequit, erit . . . applicanda lex canonica"; Gasparri, *Schema Codicis,* p. 351, c. 809: "nisi aliter iure canonico caveatur."

[16]Cf. Vromant, *De Bonis Ecclesiae,* p. 294, note 6; Wernz-Vidal, *Ius Canonicum,* IV, II, 332.

[17]Cf. M. Pistocchi, *De Re Beneficiali iuxta Canones Codicis Iuris Canonici* (Taurini: Marietti, 1928), p. 410 (hereafter cited as *De Re Beneficiali)* as to the application of French Law to the juridic nature of support received by a priest in France, and of Italian Law as to the juridic nature of support received in Italy, and Austrian Law as to the juridic nature in Austria. It is respectfully submitted that no author up to the present has fully studied and reported the effect of American Law, as Canon Law, upon the nature of support of diocesan priests in the United States.

tion whether there be any true incompatibility between the law of the place with any prescription of Divine or Canon Law must, says Cocchi, be made with great prudence.[18]

ARTICLE 2. RECOGNITION AND ENFORCEABILITY OF THE RIGHT TO SUPPORT

A. UNDER CANON LAW

1. *The Right to Support*

The delivery to diocesan priests in the United States of cash or bank checks, or other goods of value, for their support is in accordance with a right to support as granted to them by Canon Law. This right of a diocesan priest to support flows from what is called a priest's "canonical title," [19] without which canonical title a man may not receive ordination to the priesthood.[20] For diocesan priests in the United States, at the present time, the customary canonical title is the title of "service of the diocese." [21] A canonical title of a priest for his support must be both truly secure for the entire lifetime of the priest and truly sufficient for his adequate support, according to the norms given by the bishop for the diverse needs and conditions of varying times and places.[22]

---

[18]Cocchi, *Commentarium,* VI, 411; cf. Blat, *Commentarium,* IV, 546.

[19]Note that the term "title" is not univocal and has a technical meaning in American Law and at least two different technical meanings at Canon Law.

[20]Canon 974, § 1, 7°; cf. Wernz-Vidal, *Ius Canonicum,* IV, I 298; Vermeersch-Creusen, *Epitome,* II, 143-144; S. Sipos, *Enchiridion Iuris Canonici* (3 ed., Pécs: Ex Typographia "Haladás R.T.", 1936), pp. 445-448 (hereafter cited as *Enchiridion).*

[21]Ordinarily for diocesan priests the canonical title would be the title of benefice, or, in its absence, the title of patrimony or pension; Canon 979, § 1. In the United States, however, these titles are at present not in use. The title of service of the diocese is the only canonical title now in general use for diocesan priests in the United States. Cf. Wernz-Vidal, *Ius Canonicum,* IV, I, p. 298, note 310.

[22]Canon 979, § 2; Vermeersch-Creusen, *Epitome,* II, 143; Sipos, *Enchiridion,* p. 446; Wernz-Vidal, *Ius Canonicum,* IV, I, 293.

Upon every priest having the canonical title of service of the diocese there must be conferred by his bishop either a benefice, an office, or a subsidy sufficient for the priest's adequate support.[23] The duty placed upon the bishop to confer upon diocesan priests a benefice, an office, or a subsidy sufficient for their support indicates a correlative strict right at Canon Law on the part of every diocesan priest to receive truly adequate support.

2. *Enforceability of the Right to Support*

The right of diocesan priests to a fixed amount of cash support is not an absolute right, always and without exception enforceable at Canon Law.[24] As Canon Law in the United States, where during a period of many years the laity did not contribute a sufficient amount for the support of the Church and the clergy, the III Plenary Council of Baltimore, when legislating in 1884 regarding the support of diocesan priests, ordered that bishops select a fixed and definite sum which the priests could take from the funds of their assigned church for their support. This sum was given the name of *congrua* in accommodation to the ancient terminology of the Church.[25]

As a synonymous term in explanation of the word *congrua,* so that the laity could understand what was its meaning, the council by way of apposition employed the Latin word *"salarium,"* sometimes translated in English as "salary." The term "salary" as used officially in this legislation was clearly identified with the term *congrua,* whose meaning had become crystalized through centuries of usage in the Church. The priests were warned, however, "to be content with a smaller amount in case their mission or missions should be unable to supply this sum from its annual receipts." [26]

---

[23]Canon 981, § 2. cf. Wernz-Vidal, *Ius Canonicum,* IV, I, 298-299; Sipos, *Enchiridion,* p. 447; Vermeersch-Creusen, *Epitome,* II, 143-144.

[24]Cf. Canons 2303, § 2; 2304, § 2; III Plenary Council of Baltimore, Decree n. 273.

[25]D. Du Cange, *Glossarium ad Scriptores Mediae et Infimae Latinitatis* (10 vols., ed. L. Favre, Niort, 1883-1887, s.v. *Congrua* and s.v. *Portio* (hereafter cited *Glossarium).*

[26]III Plenary Council of Baltimore, Decree 273.

The bishop, *audito consultorum consilio,* was made the judge as to whether or not the mission or missions received sufficient funds from the voluntary contributions of the faithful to provide the amount needed for the support of the priests. In case the priest, for any cause, received less than the amount of the *congrua* or salary for his support, as determined by the bishop, the Canon Law of that council declared that neither the bishop nor the diocese was bound by any law whatsoever to supply the deficiency, *provided* the priest had the essential food and shelter. As late as 1941, diocesan statutes have reiterated this decree of the III Plenary Council of Baltimore as being the present law in their dioceses.[27]

Barrett has asserted that this legislation of the III Plenary Council of Baltimore continues in force today as complementing and integrating the Code of Canon Law in the United States.[28] This legislation, it is to be noted, assures the diocesan priest of the essentials of life, but likewise states that under certain circumstances anything over and above such an amount is not enforceable by the priest.[29] The Sacred Congregation for the Propagation of the Faith in 1816 had indicated similar views when, in reply to a question of the Bishop of Bardstown (Louisville) as to what was the nature of the obligation of the laity to supply support for the priests, it simply stated that the faithful are obliged "in conscience" to provide sufficient support for the priests. No mention of any enforceable obligation at law, whether Canon or secular, was made.[30] Although the Code of Canon Law legislates that the Church has a right to demand from the faithful whatever may be necessary to provide for the support of its diocesan priests,[31] it does not include legislation determining any set amount which can be enforced at Canon Law as a demand on the people for such purpose.[32]

---

[27]Cf. *Acta et Decreta Synodi Dioecesanae Toletanae Primae 1941* (Toleti: Cancelleria Curiae Dioecesanae, 1941), n. 398 (hereafter cited as *Toletana Prima).*

[28]*Comparative Study,* p. 101.

[29]Cf. F. Roberti, *Respectus Sociales in Codice Iuris Canonici* (Romae: Apollinaris, 1937), p. 50 (hereafter cited as *Respectus Sociales).*

[30]Ad 3—*Collectanea,* n. 713; *Fontes,* n. 4705.

[31]Canon 1496.

[32]Any amount enforceable "in conscience" is not herein treated. Consideration herein is limited to the factor of legal obligation.

A diocesan priest, while he has no legally enforceable right at Canon Law to receive a set salary under any and every circumstance, may receive such sum for his support when, as, and if it is available. A diocesan priest does, however, have a right enforceable at Canon Law to receive the essential food, clothing and shelter which he needs for his subsistence.[33]

Any bishop who promotes a man to the diocesan priesthood without a canonical title for support is bound to provide sufficient alimentation for the needy priest.[34] Such a bishop would, moreover, be automatically suspended from the power lawfully to promote other men to the priesthood for a period of one year, and hence would be obliged to obtain the remission of this penalty from the Holy See, or to await the lapse of a year before promoting any other men to the priesthood.[35] Not merely that bishop, but also his successors in office are obliged to provide the essentials of life for such a priest until his sustentation can otherwise be secured.[36] The Church will not recognize any pact between a bishop and a priest ordained without a title, which will prevent the priest from seeking sufficient support from the bishop personally.[37]

For the priest ordained on the title of the service of the diocese, his right to support is correlative to the duty of the bishop to confer upon him a benefice, an office, or a subsidy adequate for his support. This does not give the priest a right to any specific sum which he may enforce at Canon Law. It merely gives him a right to a sufficient support.[38]

[33]III Plenary Council of Baltimore, Decree 273; Canon 981, § 2.

[34]Canon 980, § 2; cf. Vermeersch-Creusen, *Epitome,* II, 143; Sipos, *Enchiridion,* p. 447.

[35]Canon 2373, 3°.

[36]Canon 980, § 2; cf. Sipos, *Enchiridion,* p. 447; Vermeersch-Creusen, *Epitome,* II, 143.

[37]Canon 980, § 2. In the opinion of the writer this canon represents a true example of a situation in which the American Law on Contracts and Payments would not be recognized, given effect and applied as Canon Law, since here *"aliud iure canonico cavetur."* An otherwise valid American Law contract for the conferring of an ordination without a title which at the same time involves no support obligations would not be a valid Canon Law contract. Cf. Sipos, *Enchiridion,* p. 447; Vermeersch-Creusen, *Epitome,* II, 143.

[38]Canon 981, § 2.

3. *Procedure for Enforcement of Support*

It is submitted that any diocesan priest who is not receiving an amount sufficient for his support[39] may present to his ordinary a petition setting forth all the pertinent facts and requesting additional support in view of the indication that he is *de facto* not receiving such support.[40] The petition together with the supporting evidence requires the prompt attention of the ordinary,[41] who is required to decide the matter upon having heard the advice of the diocesan consultors.[42] Any eventual recourse from an adverse administrative decision of the bishop is to be lodged with the Sacred Congregation of the Council.[43]

B. UNDER AMERICAN LAW

1. *The Right to Support*

Blackstone (1723-1780), one of the great commentators on the Common Law, based the right of priests generally to their support on the Divine Law:

---

[39]The distinction between sufficient support and the *congrua* or salary of a diocesan priest is to be borne in mind. The former he may enforce, the latter, under certain circumstances, he may not. Cf. *supra*, pp. 27-29.

[40]For further details as to the mechanics of such a petition the reader may consult J. McClunn, *Administrative Recourse,* The Catholic University of America Canon Law Studies, n. 240 (Washington, D. C.: Catholic University of America Press, 1946), pp. 41 ff.

[41]F. Schmalzgrueber, *Jus Ecclesiasticum Universum* (5 vols. in 12, Romae, 1843-1845), L. IV, tit. 39, n. 139 (hereafter cited *Jus Ecclesiasticum).*

[42]III Plenary Council of Baltimore, Decree n. 273.

[43]Cf. canon 250; McClunn *(Administrative Recourse,* pp. 41 ff.) furnishes a full explanation of the pertinent procedure. The following cases decided by the Sacred Roman Rota are of some interest on this point: 1) S.R.R., *Crediti,* 21 apr. 1910, coram R.P.D. Gustavo Persiani, Decisio XVI —*Sacrae Romanae Rotae Decisiones seu Sententiae* (Romae: Typis Polyglottis Vaticanis, 1912-), II (1910), 148-157 (hereafter cited *S.R.R. Dec.),* which followed the civil law and declared that an assistant pastor received his support under no contract whatsoever; 2) S.R.R., *Diminutionis,* 1 aug. 1911, coram R. P. D. Francisco Heiner, Dec. XXXVII—*S.R.R. Dec.,* III (1911), 413-421, which held that an assistant pastor was entitled under German civil law to receive the money paid by the government to the pastor for the assistant; 3) S.R.R., *Crediti,* 7 maii. 1936, coram R. P. D. Arcturo

> Yet an honourable and competent maintenance for the ministers of the gospel is, undoubtedly, *jure divino*, whatever the particular mode of that maintenance may be. For, besides the positive precepts of the New Testament, natural reason will tell us that an order of men, who are separate from the world and excluded from other lucrative professions for the sake of the rest of mankind, have a right to be furnished with the necessaries, conveniences, and moderate enjoyments of life at their expense for whose benefit they forego the usual means of providing them . . .[44]

Recognition of the existence of the right of diocesan priests to support presents no problem. American Law does recognize the right of priests to support.[45] Enforceability of that right at American Law is, however, a different matter.

2. *Enforceability of the Right to Support*

The right of a diocesan priest to receive delivery of cash or bank checks for his support is recognized and under certain circumstances is to a limited extent, enforceable at Canon Law. The American Law, however, as another system of law, views the matter differently. The Catholic Church cannot enact any ecclesiastical legislation which by its own force is operative in the American Secular Law. The only enforceable law in the Federal and State courts of this country is the American Secular Law. That part of the law of each state which determines whether in dealing with a legal situation the law of the Church will be recognized, given effect, or applied, may be called the law on the Conflict of Laws.[46]

Wynen, Dec. XXXII—*S.R.R. Dec.,* XXVIII (1937), 295-303, wherein a priest sued a bishop for support, and in which the Rota by turning to the civil law of Italy decreed that the bishop was not subject to any obligation to pay the priest the so-called salary so long as the priest had already received a sufficient support.

[44]Blackstone, *Commentaries on the Laws of England* (12 ed., 4 vols., Dublin, 1775), Book II, Section 25 (hereafter cited as *Commentaries).*

[45]*Tuigg v. Sheehan,* 101 Pa. 363 (1882).

[46]Cf. *Restatement of the Law of Conflict of Laws* (St. Paul: American Law Institute Publishers, 1934), p. 1 (hereafter cited as *Restatement of Conflict of Laws).* Canon Law itself has a number of canons which de-

It is a fundamental principle of the American Law of Conflict of Laws that no state will directly enforce a duty to support as created by the law of another state.[47] From this it may be inferred that no state will directly enforce a duty created only by the law of the Church in requiring the support of priests. A sound principle of Inter-Church-and-State Common Law is in accord. Furthermore, the Constitution of the United States determines that the free exercise of religion will not be *affirmatively* secured, but that nevertheless it must not be infringed. It was to be secured by a liberty, by a condition of *legal hands off*.[48] Therefore the State and Federal Courts have no jurisdiction to enforce rights to support which are given only by the Church.

To be enforceable under American Law, any right to support as enjoyed by a priest must have been given him by the American Law itself. Generally considered, the duty to support a person is imposed by the state as an enforcement of its own public policy. Its enforcement is of no special interest to other states and, since the duty is not imposed primarily for the benefit of an individual, it is not enforceable under the principles of the Conflict of Laws if given by another system of law.[49] A state will, however, indirectly enforce even such a duty to give support by enforcing a quasi-contractual duty.[50]

In the case of *Tuigg v. Sheehan*[51] the Reverend Patrick M. Sheehan brought an action against the Right Reverend John Tuigg, Bishop of the Diocese of Pittsburgh, to recover $2,400.00 allegedly

---

termine when the law of the place will be recognized, given effect and applied as Canon Law in a given situation. As examples, and not as an all-inclusive list, there may be mentioned here Canons 1080; 1499, § 1; 1508; 1523; 1529; 1539, § 1; 1538, § 1; 1542, § 2; 1543; cf. cc. 1509, 1°; 1926; 1795; 1813, § 2; 1930; 1933, § 3; 2223, § 3, 2°. Cf. Roberti, *Respectus Sociales*, p. 50.

[47] *Restatement of Conflict of Laws*, p. 458.

[48] O'Brien, "Freedom of Religion in Restatement of Inter-Church-and-State Common Law," *The Jurist*, VI (1946), 508-509.

[49] *Restatement of Conflict of Laws*, § 458, a.

[50] *Restatement of Conflict of Laws*, § 458, b.

[51] 101 Pa. 363 (1882).

due him for his support. The American court, taking notice of the Canon Law right of a diocesan priest to receive support, said:

> Had the plaintiff [Father Sheehan] sought redress within his church, his rights would have been determined by the laws of the church.

The Court then proceeded to add:

> When, however, he seeks aid of the civil courts, he is to be treated precisely as any other citizen and his rights are to be determined by the same standard [the American Law standard].

The Court in this case of *Tuigg v. Sheehan* reasoned:

> All that can be . . . claimed is that the church is bound by its own organic law to provide decent support for its priests. That it is a duty of a religious denomination to provide a support for its teachers is a fact that is recognized with few exceptions all over Christendom. It is said, however, to be especially binding upon the Catholic Church for the reason that its priests are debarred by its canons . . . from engaging in any secular employment. . . . However binding such a duty may be *in foro conscientiae,* when it comes to its enforcement in a court of law, the plaintiff must show a contract.

3. *Procedure for Enforcement of Support*

There is no procedure whatsoever at American Law whereby a diocesan priest may enforce his Canon Law right to support. Various attempts have been made by priests to enforce support, but in each and every case without exception the American courts of last resort have held that the diocesan priest is without any legal remedy, at American Law, for his support.[52] The law stands ever ready to enforce any contract which a priest may have for his support. The priest, however, has entered into a relation in his Church, which by its very nature excludes all possibility of a contract.[53]

---

[52]*Tuigg. v. Sheehan,* 101 Pa. 363 (1882); *Rose v. Vertin,* 46 Mich. 457 (1881); *Baxter v. McDonnell,* 155 N.Y. 83 (1898).

[53]C. Zollmann, *American Church Law* (St. Paul: West Publishing Co., 1933), p. 453.

Article 3. Canon 1529 Adopts American Law as to Contracts and Payments in the United States for the Nature of Support of Diocesan Priests

The present law of the Church is that the law of the place as to contracts and payments is recognized, given effect, and applied by the Code of Canon Law *as Canon Law.*[54] In two cases only the Church does not adopt the law of the place as Canon Law on contracts and payments. If the law of the place be contrary to the Divine Law, then Canon Law does not adopt such civil law. If the law of the place be contrary to an express provision of Canon Law, whether general or particular, then such civil law is not adopted as Canon Law.[55]

It is submitted, and an examination of the Canon Law and the American Law as previously set forth in Article 2 of this Chapter will indicate, that there is nothing in the American Law, in respect to the nature of the support of diocesan priests contrary to the Divine Law. On the contrary, American Common Law, following the English Common Law, bases the right of priests generally to receive support upon the Divine Law.[56] The American Law makes no provisions contrary to the universal Canon Law of the Code of Canon Law as to the support of diocesan priests. Instead it recognizes the right of priests to receive their support, and by a policy of *legal hands off* leaves the entire matter up to the Church.[57] The American Law makes no provisions contrary to the particular Canon Law of the United States as expressed in the Baltimore

---

[54]Canon 1529; Vromant, *De Bonis Ecclesiae,* p. 291; J. Cleary, *The Canonical Limitations on the Alienation of Church Property,* The Catholic University of America Canon Law Studies, n. 100 (Washington, D. C.: Catholic University of America, 1936), p. 10, (hereafter cited as *Limitations on Alienation).*

[55]Cocchi, *Commentarium,* VI, 410-411; Blat, *Commentarium,* IV, 545-546; Berutti, *Institutiones,* IV, 509, especially note 1; Vermeersch-Creusen, *Epitome,* II, 485; Wernz-Vidal, *Ius Canonicum,* IV, II, 331-332; cf. S.R.R., *Crediti,* 21 mart. 1931, coram R. P. D. Massimo Massimi, Dec. XII—*S.R.R. Dec.,* XXIII (1931), 92-101.

[56]Blackstone, *Commentaries,* Book II, Section 25.

[57]Cf. *Tuigg* v. *Sheehan,* 101 Pa. 363 (1882); Heston, *Alienation,* pp. 65-66.

Councils. It leaves the matter exclusively within the jurisdiction of the Church.[58]

Accordingly it is submitted that, as to the nature of the support of diocesan priests in the United States, the provision of canon 1529 in adopting the American Law as to contracts and payments is *the Canon Law in the United States.* As a result, the Church recognizes, gives effect to, and applies the American Law on contracts and payments as the Canon Law with reference to the nature of support of diocesan priests in the United States.[59]

---

[58]Heston, *Alienation,* p. 67.

[59]Cf. Heston, *Alienation,* pp. 66-68. Note that, as to enforceability of the right to support, Canon Law does not adopt the American Law which never permits enforcement, unless there be an American Law contract, but provides on the contrary for a limited enforceability, not indeed by contract or quasi-contract, but simply in consequence of an enacted ecclesiastical canon. This canon Secular Law in its turn will not recognize, apply, or enforce.

Chapter IV

CONTRACTS AND PAYMENTS AT AMERICAN CANON LAW

Article 1. Preliminary Notions

The essential constituents of a contract are in the United States identical at Canon Law and at American Law. This identity in the two systems of law results from the adoption and canonization as it were by Canon Law of the American Law on contracts and payments.[1] Canon 1529 is a momentous canon.[2] Because of canon 1529, the American Law *must* be observed as the Canon Law in the United States as to contracts and payments.[3] As a result of the adoption by Canon Law of the American Law of contracts, the Canon Law in the United States will differ, as to contracts and as to payments, from the Canon Law in various European countries which follow the old Roman and the modern Civil Law.[4]

In their treatment of canon 1529 most of the commentators seem confused. Some of them merely quote the canon and then attempt to explain it by drawing upon various passages from Roman Law, and from the Italian, French, German, and other Civil Codes.[5]

---

[1]Canon 1529—Quae ius civile in territorio statuit de contractibus tam in genere, quam in specie, sive nominatis sive innominatis, et de solutionibus, eadem iure canonico in materia ecclesiastica iisdem cum effectibus serventur, nisi iuri divino contraria sint aut aliud iure canonico caveatur.

[2]Vermeersch-Creusen, *Epitome,* II, 485.

[3]Cocchi, *Commentarium,* VI, 410-411.

[4]Vromant, *De Bonis Ecclesiae,* pp. 289-291; cf. R. Pound, "A Comparison of the Ideals of Law," *HLR,* XLVII (1933), 1, at p. 11, cited *supra,* p. 24, n. 11.

[5]Cf. as examples, but not as an all-inclusive listing, F. Cappello, *Summa Iuris Canonici* (ed. 2, 3 vols., Romae: apud Aedes Universitatis Gregorianae, 1932-1940), II, 577-578 (hereafter cited as *Summa*); Berutti, *Institutiones,* IV, 508-510; A. De Meester, *Juris Canonici et Juris Canonico-civilis Compendium* (3 vols in 4, ed. nova, Brugis: Desclée de Brouwer et Si,

Vromant states that priests should consult the legal experts of their respective regions.[6] Wernz (1842-1914)-Vidal (1868-1939) stated that the treatment of contracts and payments must be sought in the commentators on the law of the respective place.[7]

It is submitted that those European commentators who quote the canon itself and then attempt to give a definition of a contract and to lay down conditions such as ***habilitas contrahentium, materia apta, consensus validus,*** and ***causa,*** citing either Roman Law or European Civil Codes as authorities for the explanation, cannot rightly be used in the treatment of canon 1529 *as it applies in the United States of America.* It is submitted that Vromant and Wernz-Vidal, in stating that the legal experts and the most authoritative commentators of the law in the respective regions should be consulted, point the way to a true and accurate interpretation of canon 1529 in its application for the United States of America.[8]

No official interpretation of canon 1529 has been issued by the Pontifical Commission for the Authentic Interpretation of the Canons of the Code, as of January 1, 1949.[9] In the absence of any official interpretation of this canon, as an indication of the correct manner of its application, from which in turn further principles of interpretation could be drawn, a search has been made of every case decided by the Sacred Roman Rota from May 19, 1918, the effective date of that canon, to the latest published volume of the Rotal Decisions. Thirteen cases involving the application of canon 1529 have been decided by the Sacred Roman Rota.

In a Neapolitan case[10] it was stated that canon 1529 began to have force on May 19, 1918, and that contracts entered into prior to that date were to be considered as governed by the previous

---

1921-1928), III, I, 400-401 (hereafter cited as *Compendium*) ; E. Regatillo, *Institutiones Iuris Canonici* (2 vols., Santander: Sal Terrae, 1941-1942), II, 141 (hereafter cited as *Institutiones*) ; Sipos, *Enchiridion*, p. 789.

[6] *De Bonis Ecclesiae*, p. 294.

[7] *Ius Canonicum*, IV, II, 332.

[8] Cf. Blat, *Commentarium*, IV, 546.

[9] Cf. T. Bouscaren, *The Canon Law Digest* (2 vols., Milwaukee: Bruce Publishing Co., 1934-1943) as traced to date in the *AAS*.

[10] S.R.R., *Crediti et Refectionis Damnorum*, 10 dec. 1926, coram R. P. D. Francisco Parrillo, Dec. XLVIII—*S. R. R. Dec.*, XVIII (1926), 386-403.

legislation in accordance with the prescription of canon 10. Therefore the Rota applied the pre-Code legislation to this 1914 contract.

In a second case[11] it was stated that canon 1529 was not to be so strictly interpreted that ecclesiastical judges could never depart from the secular law in trials involving contracts or payments.

In a third case[12] a controversy had arisen regarding a contract entered into in France. The Rotal Decision declared that the cause had to be tried according to the norms of the French Civil Law on contracts. Immediately, in order to determine the nature and character of a contract and of its essential elements in France, the Tribunal turned to the pertinent provisions of the French Civil Code. No consideration whatsoever was given to Roman Law or to any of the so-called "standard Canon Law commentators." The French Civil Code was pointed to as the only source for an ascertainment of the essential elements of a Canon Law contract in France. The decision was indeed appealed, but not on the plea of any improper application of canon 1529 in the case. The opinion on the appeal was delivered on July 11, 1928.

In a fourth case[13] a controversy existed regarding a payment to be made in France. The opinion of the Tribunal was that canon 1529 required that the French Law be recognized, given effect, and applied in the case. The opinion then designated the respective ruling in the French Civil Law as the *proper Canon Law* applicable in the case. An appeal was taken to the Apostolic Signatura, which upheld the Rotal Decision.

In the rehearing of a case which had been appealed from an earlier sentence of the Rota a new panel of auditors *(turnus)* of the Sacred Roman Rota[14] declared that the prescription of canon

---

[11] S.R.R., *Restitutionis in Integrum et Compromissi,* 5 iul. 1927, coram R. P. D. Francisco Parrillo, Dec. XXXIV—*S. R. R. Dec.,* XIX (1927), 276-298, esp. 292-293.

[12] S. R. R., *Crediti,* 5 iul. 1927, coram R. P. D. Andrea Jullien, Dec. XXXIII—*S. R. R. Dec.,* XIX (1927), 261-275.

[13] S. R. R., *Recuperandae Possessionis,* 30 iul. 1927, coram R. P. D. Francisco Guglielmi, Dec. XLI—*S. R. R. Dec.,* XIX (1927), 357-362.

[14] S. R. R., *Crediti,* 11 iul. 1928, coram R. P. D. Francisco Parrillo, Dec. XXXII—*S. R. R. Dec.* XX (1928), 292-305. This is the rehearing of the case noted above as the third case. *S. R. R. Dec.* XIX (1927), 261-275.

1529 required that the Tribunal recognize, give effect to, and apply the French Law on contracts as the Canon Law. The Tribunal again turned to the various articles of the French Civil Code regarding the essential elements of a contract and the invalidating provisions of the French Civil Law on contracts. It may be noted that in interpreting the various articles of the French Civil Code the Sacred Roman Rota turned to and cited various cases as decided in the French Civil Courts, and employed the rendered decisions as declaratory of the Canon Law in the case. Once again the decision of the Rota was appealed, but not on the claim of any misapplication of the import of canon 1529. The Apostolic Signatura, on February 3, 1930, granted a *restitutio in integrum,* that is, restored the litigated case to its original status, and thereupon the case again reached the Sacred Roman Rota on March 21, 1931.

In a new hearing of this case,[15] with all the auditors sitting *en banc,* the Rota declared that the Canon Law regarding a contract entered into in France had to be derived exclusively from the rules of the French Civil Code and as interpreted by the French Civil Law experts. The Rota did not take into account any other sources than the French law and its commentators in reaching the decision which then stood as the definitive sentence *(sententia transiit in rem iudicatam).*

In a case, heard in 1931,[16] which involved the payment of money allegedly due, it was declared by the Sacred Roman Rota that under canon 1529 the German law, known as the *Aufwertungagesetz,* had to be applied as the *Canon Law,* relevant in the case. No reference whatsoever was made to any Roman Law or to any of the standard commentators on Canon Law. Instead, all reference was to the German laws and the commentators thereon.

A 1932 case[17] involved the payment of money in Italy. The Tribunal stated that under canon 1529 the Canon Law in the case was the Italian law as taken from the Italian Civil Code.

[15]S. R. R., *Crediti,* 21 mart. 1931, coram omnibus auditoribus, Dec. XII—*S. R. R. Dec.,* XXIII (1931), 92-100.

[16]S. R. R., *Crediti,* 4 maii 1931, coram R. P. D. Ubaldo Mannucci, Dec. XXI—*S.R.R. Dec.,* XXIII (1931), 164-171.

[17]S. R. R., *Solutionis,* 10 dec. 1932, coram R. P. D. Andrea Jullien, Dec. LIV—*S.R.R. Dec.,* XXIV (1932), 504-517.

Another 1932 case[18] involved the effects of a contract in Italy. The Tribunal stated that the Italian Civil Law was the Canon Law in the case, and immediately turned to the pertinent articles of the Italian Civil Code. This case was appealed and a sentence was then rendered on August 3, 1934. Upon a further appeal the Apostolic Signatura on December 7, 1935 granted a *restitutio in integrum.* The matter has not been resubmitted since then for a hearing by the Rota. But the earlier appeals did not in any way call into question the manner in which canon 1529 had been applied in the case.

In a 1936 case[19] which involved a contract, the Tribunal declared that under canon 1529 the Canon Law was to be found in the Italian Civil Code, which it adopted and applied. With reference to the manner of establishing judicial proof, however, not the Italian law, but the law as contained in Book IV of the Code of Canon Law regarding witnesses was followed. In this case a previous Rotal Decision[20] was cited with approval as authority for the proposition that canon 1529 required the exclusive recognition and application as Canon Law of the Italian Civil Code for a contract entered into in Italy.

Another 1936 case[21] involved a contract entered into in Italy. The Tribunal applied canon 1529 by turning to the *Codice Civile del Regno d'Italia* as the Canon Law on contracts and payments. No mention was made of any of the standard Canon Law commentators; all terms were taken from and defined solely in accord with the Italian Civil Code.

In a third 1936 case[22] the Tribunal declared that in a controversy regarding a contract made in Switzerland the Canon Law of the

[18] S. R. R., *Crediti,* 21 dec. 1932, coram R. P. D. Francisco Guglielmi, Dec. LVIII—*S. R. R. Dec.,* XXIV (1932), 539-557.

[19] S. R. R., *Locationis Operis et Damnorum,* 16 nov. 1936, coram R. P. D. Andrea Jullien, Dec. LXXII—*S. R. R. Dec.,* XXVIII (1936), 680-693.

[20] S. R. R., *Crediti et Refectionis Damnorum,* 10 dec. 1926, coram R. P. D. Francisco Parrillo, Dec. XLVIII—*S. R. R. Dec.* XVIII (1926), 386-403. Cf. *supra,* p. 37.

[21] S. R. R., *Iurium et Possessionis,* 4 apr. 1936, coram R. P. D. Andrea Jullien, Dec. XXI—*S. R. R. Dec.* XXVIII (1936), 196-207.

[22] S. R. R., *Redditionis Rationum et Exsecutionis Sententiae,* 30 maii 1936, coram R. P. D. Andrea Jullien, Dec. XXXVII—*S. R. R. Dec.,* XXVIII (1936), 349-358.

Church was such that French or Italian laws were in no way applicable as Canon Law to this case, but that the Swiss laws on contracts and payments were to be recognized, given effect, and applied as the Canon Law.

In a 1937 case[23] which involved a contract entered into in Italy, the Tribunal declared that the controversy had to be decided according to the norm of canon 1529, which required that the Italian Civil Code be recognized, given effect and applied as Canon Law. The Tribunal then cited the various applicable articles from the Italian Civil Code. It may be noted that in construing the meaning of the various articles of the Italian Civil Code, the Sacred Roman Rota turned to a number of decisions of the Italian Supreme Tribunal "di Cassazione" and applied them as decisions affecting Canon Law.

From this examination of all the Rotal cases which involved the application of canon 1529, certain principles appear to be clear as to the meaning of this canon. The Auditors of the Sacred Roman Rota, learned in the law and in the interpretation thereof, have evidently acquiesced in the suggestion of Vromant and Wernz-Vidal that for a proper understanding of canon 1529, when in contractual matters the local Civil Law is appropriated as the local Canon Law, the legal experts of the respective regions should be consulted and followed. They have sedulously avoided the approach of certain Canon Law commentators, according to whom the Roman or Modern Civil Law is always stressed as a controlling factor. They have in each case turned to the law of the place of the contract or payment, and have used that law as the Canon Law.

For interpretations of that law the Auditors have taken the decisions of the courts of the States in question. No reported case involving canon 1529 as applicable in the United States of America has reached the Sacred Roman Rota. Applying the principles as drawn from the application of canon 1529 by the Auditors of the Sacred Roman Rota over a period of nearly twenty-five years, the present writer elects to turn to the American Law and the American legal experts thereon as constituting the Canon Law and the Canon

[23] S. R. R., *Crediti et Damnorum*, 24 febr. 1937, coram Excmo. P. D. Julio Grazioli, Decano, Dec. XIV—*S. R. R. Dec.*, XXIX (1937), 116-148.

Law commentators for his treatment of this canon as it affects the nature of support of diocesan priests in the United States of America.

It is vitally important that representatives of the Canon Law bear in mind the need of exercising the utmost care and caution when they interpret the law of the Church as expressed by moral theologians with reference to contracts in the United States of America and in relation to the nature of support of diocesan priests in the United States. The Canon Law on contracts and payments in this country may differ from the alleged moral theology on contracts and payments as advanced by European theologians, since their system of doctrine in classifying contracts and the elements inherent in them is based upon European secular law and jurisprudence.[24]

The Canon Law on contracts and payments in the United States likewise obviously differs from the Canon Law on contracts and payments in the various European countries. Hence the need for extreme care in the use of non-American authors and laws in determining the nature of support of diocesan priests in the United States. The warning of Blat must be borne in mind:

> Canonists must learn the law of each nation on contracts. . . . It is *only* from a canonist who is expert in this matter that the solution of specific cases can be *prudently* expected, though in addition a considerable sagacity will at times be needed if one is properly to differentiate a true opposition between these systems of law from an opposition which is only apparent.[25]

---

[24]Compare A. Vermeersch, *Theologia Moralis* (3 ed., 4 vols., Roma: Pontificia Universita Gregoriana, Reimpressio, 1945) II, 297-300, with *Restatement of the Law of Contracts* (2 vols., St. Paul: American Law Institute Publishers, 1932), I, 1-15 (hereafter cited as *Restatement of Contracts);* and compare H. Noldin-A. Schmidt, *Summa Theologiae Moralis* (27 ed., 3 vols., Oeniponte/Lipsiae: Sumptibus et Typis Feliciani Rauch, 1940-1941), II, 481-486, with R. Pound, "A Comparison of the Ideals of Law," *HLR,* XLVII (1933), 1, in which it is indicated that, though a transaction is a transaction at Rome and Washington, yet the legal understanding and treatment of the transaction in the two places may be very different.

[25]*Commentarium,* IV, 546. Translation and italics by writer.

ARTICLE 2. CONSTITUENT ELEMENTS IN THE CONCEPT OF "CONTRACT"

A contract at Canon Law in the United States is a promise, or a set of promises, for the breach of which the law gives a remedy, or the performance of which the law in some way recognizes as a duty.[26] The essential elements of a contract at Canon Law in the United States are: (1) Parties competent to contract; (2) a subject matter; (3) a legally sufficient consideration; (4) mutuality of agreement; and (5) mutuality of obligation.[27] Inasmuch as under American Law no *restrictions* are placed upon the capacity of priests to contract, upon contracts whereby ministers of religion receive their support, or regarding mutuality of agreement and of obligation, in the measure in which these may relate to the nature of the support of diocesan priests, no further treatment thereon is deemed necessary in this study.[28]

It is requisite in American Law for the formation of a contract that a *legally sufficient consideration* be given for the promise or promises therein. This doctrine finds no close analogy in the Roman or modern Civil Law followed by European Canon Law.[29] There is a sharp distinction between *causa* in Roman or modern Civil Law

[26]*Restatement of Contracts,* I, 1; S. Williston, *A Treatise on the Law of Contracts* (8 vols., New York: Baker, Voorhis & Co., 1936), I, § 1 (hereafter cited as *Contracts).* It is to be noted that these works constitute true Canon Law commentaries in the United States, although not in certain European countries which follow the modern Civil Law. Williston as the greatest commentator on contracts in American Law is consequently the greatest Canon Law commentator on contracts at Canon Law in the United States. Cf. Vromant, *De Bonis Ecclesiae,* p. 294; Wernz-Vidal, *Ius Canonicum,* IV, II, 332; Blat, *Commentarium,* IV, 546.

[27]Williston, *Contracts,* I, §§ 17-21; § 22-§ 137A. *Corpus Juris, Being a Complete and Systematic Statement of the Whole Body of the Law,* edited by William Mack, LL.D., and Donald J. Kiser, LL.D. (71 vols., New York: The American Law Book Co., 1914-1935), 13, pp. 237-238 (hereafter cited C.J.).

[28]For a more complete treatment of the whole subject of contracts consult 13 C.J., s.v. "Contract," and for a comparison with European Canon Law contracts consult 13 C.J., s.v. "Contratos." Indirect restrictions as to the amounts which donors may give or bequeath to priests, since they have no bearing upon the nature of the support, are not herein discussed.

[29]Cf. Berutti, *Institutiones,* IV, 509; Williston, *Contracts,* I, 99.

and *consideration* in *American* Canon Law. *Causa* denotes some adequate reason for making a promise, and may be either a present exchange or an existing state of facts. Consideration is a present exchange bargained for in return for a promise. Williston states that there is no close analogy between the two.[30]

The fundamental idea is that the consideration is the exchange or price requested and received by the promisor for the promise. It is, in substance, a detriment incurred by the promisee at the request of the promisor as the price for the promise, or the benefit received by the promisor. Benefit and detriment have technical meanings. Detriment, as used in a test of the sufficiency of a consideration, points to a legal detriment as distinguished from a detriment in fact. It means giving up something which immediately prior thereto the promisee was privileged to keep on doing, or refraining from something which he then was privileged to do. And benefit correspondingly must mean the receiving as the exchange for his promise of some performance or forbearance which the promisor was not previously entitled to receive.[31]

Consideration relates to the essence of a contract. A thing is not a consideration if it is not regarded as such by both parties.[32] It is not everything which is requested or given in exchange for a promise that will make the promise enforceable. In other words, not everything which the parties agree upon as a consideration will be treated by the law as a *legally sufficient consideration.*[33] Consideration, to be legally sufficient, means something which is of value in the eye of the law.[34]

In addition to the adoption into Canon Law by virtue of canon 1529 of the legal principles of consideration embodied in the Common Law, such valid secular *statutory* provisions involving con-

---

[30]*Contracts,* I, § 111; *Restatement of Contracts,* I, § 80, sqq.

[31]Williston, *Contracts,* I, § 102, § 102A.

[32]*McGovern v. City of N. Y.,* 234 N. Y. 377, 388; 138 N. E. 26, 31; cf. S. R. R., *Crediti,* 11 iul. 1928, coram R. P. D. Francisco Parrillo, Dec. XXXII—*S.R.R. Dec.* XX (1928), 292-305, as to the application as Canon Law under canon 1529 of the law of the place regarding the invalidity of contracts.

[33]Williston, *Contracts,* I, § 101; *Restatement of Contracts,* § 81.

[34]*Thomas v. Thomas,* 2 Q. B. 851, by Mr. Justice Patterson.

tracts and payments which do not contravene Federal or State constitutions and which do not contravene the Divine Law and any express provision of the Canon Law, whether general or particular in a given territory, are also recognized and adopted as part of Canon Law, as for example, the pertinent provisions of the Federal Gift Tax Law, section 1002 of which provides:

> "Transfer for less than adequate and full consideration. Where property is transferred for less than an adequate and full consideration in money or money's worth, then the amount by which the value of the property exceeded the value of the consideration shall, for the purpose of the tax imposed by this chapter, be deemed a gift, and shall be included in computing the amount of gifts made during the calendar year. 53 Stat. 146."

Construing this section the Supreme Court of the United States,[35] in two cases decided in 1945,[36] declared that the facts warranted findings that property had been transferred "for less than an adequate and full consideration in money or money's worth" and concluded that gifts had been made. The Court said, in one of the cases:

> "Congress intended to use the term 'gift' in its broadest and most comprehensive sense."

It would seem, in Federal gift tax cases, that a consideration not reducible to a money value is to be wholly disregarded in contracts that involve a payment of money, which money thereby ceases to be received by reason of a contract, but is received rather by reason of a gift.[37]

[35]Cf. S. R. R., *Crediti,* 24 febr. 1937, coram Excmo P. D. Julio Grazioli, Decano, Dec. XIV—*S. R. R. Dec.,* XIX (1937), 116-148, as an example wherein the Sacred Roman Rota interpreted an article of the Italian Civil Code, constituted as Canon Law by the norm of canon 1529, by citing decisions of the Italian Supreme Tribunal "di Cassazione" and applying the civil decision *as Canon Law;* and S. R. R., *Crediti,* 11 iul. 1928, *supra,* in which the French Tribunals of last resort were cited as interpretative of the French Canon Law on contracts and payments.

[36]*Commissioner v. Wemyss,* 324 U. S. 303, 89 L. ed. 958 (1945). *Merrill v. Fahs,* 324 U. S. 308, 89 L. ed. 963 (1945).

[37]*United States Code* (1946 ed., 50 Titles, Washington, D. C.: United States Government Printing Office, 1947) Title 26, § 1002 (hereafter cited

With reference to the nature of support of diocesan priests in the United States of America and its basis in any legally sufficient consideration in the form of an adequate and full consideration that can be valued in "money or money's worth," it is fitting to recall the canons on simony. The studious intention of buying or selling for a temporal price any intrinsically spiritual thing, or any temporal thing annexed to the spiritual in such a manner that the spiritual thing is even the partial object of a contract, is simony in the Divine Law.[38] The provision of Canon 728 prohibits a contract even as long as from the circumstances it may be inferred that a temporal price has been put on a spiritual thing.[39]

Canonists must, therefore, use extreme care in determining whether or not there is any legally sufficient consideration measurable in money or money's worth in the nature of support of diocesan priests, lest there be any violation of the Divine Law prohibiting simony.[40] To be sure, there is no simony when a temporal price is not paid for the spiritual thing, but is given upon the occasion thereof under a just title or in consequence of a legitimate custom.[41]

The *Restatement of Contracts,* instead of defining the requisites of a legally sufficient consideration affirmatively has defined them negatively. In other words, it has adopted the more liberal approach of recognizing that primarily the parties determine the actual consideration by making it the thing agreed upon as that which is to

---

U.S.C.); *The Code of Federal Regulations of The United States of America* (15 vols. in 17 & Index, Washington, D. C.: United States Government Printing Office, 1939) Title 26, Cumulative Supplement, § 86.8 (hereafter cited as CFR and, with Cumulative Supplement, as CFR, Cum. Supp.).

[38]Canon 727, § 1; Sipos, *Enchiridion,* pp. 416-417; Vermeersch-Creusen, *Epitome,* II, 2-5; R. Ryder, *Simony,* The Catholic University of America Canon Law Studies, n. 65 (Washington, D. C.: The Catholic University of America, 1931) p. 101.

[39]Sipos, *Enchiridion,* pp. 417-418; Vermeersch-Creusen, *Epitome,* II, 3; Canon 728.

[40]Cf. Blat, *Commentarium,* IV, 546.

[41]Canon 730; cf. J. Richardson, *The Just Title in Canon 730 for giving something temporal on the occasion of the Sacred Ministry* (Rome: Institutum Pontificium Internationale Angelicum, 1936), p. 16 (hereafter cited as *Just Title).*

be given in exchange for the promise, and that secondarily the law will give effect thereto unless that thing given in exchange has been held legally insufficient.[42] Motive is not the same thing as consideration.[43] Moral obligation is not a legally sufficient consideration.[44]

A doctrine formerly prevailed that an express promise motivated by a previously existing moral obligation furnished a sufficient consideration to create a valid contract. But it is obvious that a promise motivated exclusively by a sense of moral obligation is simply a matter of voluntary action; and it is now settled in accordance with the general rule that no valid contract arises from it. At the present day there can be no doubt that the doctrine which regards moral consideration as a factor that suffices for the making of a contract is wholly discredited.[45] Hence the statements of moral theologians concerning the obligations, rights, and duties, *in conscience,* regarding the support of diocesan priests are of no current legal force at Canon Law in the United States regarding the nature of support of diocesan priests.[46]

The law in most of the United States has rejected the principle of a purely moral consideration, and there can be no question that in most states a plaintiff would invite disaster if he endeavored to support an action in the secular courts on the theory that the promise was supported indeed by a moral consideration but with nothing more. Though the doctrine which warrants the sufficiency of a moral consideration in a contract is generally discredited as American Law, it still survives in a few states, namely in Louisiana, Illinois, Maryland, Michigan, and Pennsylvania.[47]

Every true contract is enforceable by a judicial action. Contracts at Canon Law in the United States can be express or implied. An express contract is one in which the intention of the parties and the terms of the agreement are declared or expressed by the parties

---

[42]§§ 75, 76, ff.; cf. Williston, *Contracts,* I, § 99 ff.

[43]*Thomas* v. *Thomas,* 2 Q. B. 851; cf. O'Brien and O'Brien, "How New York Restricts Gifts for Masses," *Fordham Law Review,* XIII (1044), 175, at 188 ff.

[44]Williston, *Contracts,* I §§ 147-148.

[45]Williston, *Contracts,* I, § 147.

[46]Cf. *supra,* Chapter III, p. 21.

[47]Williston, *Contracts,* I, §§ 148-149.

in writing or orally at the time the contract is entered into.[48] An implied contract may be: (1) implied in fact, or (2) implied in law. In the case of contracts implied in fact, there must be an assent of the parties as in express contracts, while in the case of contracts implied in law, or more properly called quasi-contracts, the obligation arises not from the consent of the contractants but from the law or natural equity.[49]

Contracts implied in fact show a mutual intent to contract. Contracts implied in law, or quasi-contracts, constitute a class of obligations which are created by law, not in consequence of the consent of the party who is bound, but on the ground that they are dictated by reason and justice, and thus they lend themselves to becoming enforced by an action *quasi ex contractu*. They rest solely on a legal fiction; the obligation arises, not from consent, but from the law.[50]

There are only two alternatives at American Law, and for that very reason also at Canon Law in the United States, in accordance with which money or property received by a diocesan priest for his support can be classified according to its nature: compensation or gift.[51] These two concepts are mutually exclusive, and any bestowal

[48] 13 C.J., 240.

[49] 13 C.J., 240-241.

[50] 13 C.J., 244.

[51] The classification of capital gains under the Federal, State and Municipal tax laws is by its own definition inapplicable to the support of diocesan priests from ecclesiastical sources. By an Act of Congress, non-contractual support received by civil and military officers of the government is legally treated as if it were a contractual compensation (cf. 26 U.S.C. p. 2530-2531). Prior to this act said sums were not deemed contractual compensation subject to the provisions of 26 U.S.C. § 22a as taxable income. No such statute has been enacted to change the legal treatment of the nature of support of diocesan priests from the Common Law classifications of compensation or gift into an arbitrary statutory classification.

By a regulation the Treasury Department, Bureau of Internal Revenue, has attempted to transfer Mass stipends and stole fees from the Canon Law-Common Law classification as of the nature of a gift into a category which would purport to make them to be of the nature of compensation. (26 CFR, Cum. Supp., § 29.22.) Such regulation does not necessarily have the force of law (*M. E. Blatt Co.* v. *U. S.*, 305 U. S. 267). In the only reported case in which such a regulation (herein by a municipal officer

of support must be either the one or the other.[52] It cannot be both.

The case of *Bogardus v. Commissioner of Internal Revenue* is the leading case regarding the differentiation between these two concepts. In the course of the opinion of the United States Supreme Court, Mr. Justice Sutherland (1862-1942) declared:

> . . . the Statute [an American tax law] definitely distinguishes between compensation on the one hand and gifts on the other hand, the former being taxable and the latter free from taxation [under income tax laws]. The two terms are, and were meant to be, mutually exclusive; and a bestowal of money cannot, under the statute, be both a gift and a payment of compensation . . .

---

under authority of a municipality) has been subject to judicial review the court decided that it did not have the force of reclassifying Mass stipends and stole fees as contractual compensation from their classification as gifts under both American Common Law and Canon Law. *(Ross* v. *City of Philadelphia,* 25 A 2d 834) (cf. J. Mertens, *The Law of Federal Income Taxation* [12 vols., Chicago: Callaghan and Co., 1942], I, § 8.04 [hereinafter cited as *Taxation*]).

There remains accordingly at American Law—both Canon and Secular—only the twofold possible alternative classification, compensation or gift, under which the *nature* of the support of diocesan priests in the United States may be classified.

[52]It is to be noted that the terms generally utilized with reference to the support of diocesan priests are not univocal. For example, Schmalzgrueber (L. IV, tit. 39, n. 122) spoke of the support received by diocesan priests as a "remuneration." Remuneration, at American Canon Law, can be and is used to designate both compensation and a gift, *causa remunerationis* (51 C.J., 124). A remunerative gift is *a gift,* the object of which is to recompense for services rendered (Cf. 12 C.J., 229, 231). It is possible for money to be transferred to a priest with a motive of remuneration, and yet without any intent to make a contract involving all the legal consequences of a contract, and without a legally sufficient consideration whereby a contract would come into being so as to change the nature of the transaction from a gift to compensation. It is further possible for money to be transferred to a priest with the described motive without the result of a quasi-contract because of the legal "hands off" policy of the American Law regarding the support of diocesan priests. Cf. O'Brien and O'Brien, "Freedom of Religion in Restatement of Inter-Church-and-State Common Law," *The Jurist,* VI (1946), 503-523; R. Pound, "A Comparison of the Ideals of Law," *HLR* XLVII (1933), 1, at p. 11; *Bogardus* v. *Commissioner of Internal Revenue,* 302 U. S. 34 (1937).

> If the sum of money under consideration was a gift and not compensation, it is exempt from taxation and cannot be made taxable by resort to any form of subclassification. If it be in fact a gift, that is an end of the matter; and inquiry whether it be a gift of one sort or another is irrelevant. This is necessarily true, for since all gifts are made non-taxable [under income tax laws], there can be no such thing under the [income tax] statute as a taxable gift. A *claim* that it is a gift presents the sole and simple question whether its designation as such is genuine or fictitious . . . that is to say, whether though called a gift, it is *in reality* compensation. To determine that question we turn to the facts . . .

The fact to be determined is merely whether or not there is in reality a contract, express or implied, or a quasi-contract, whereby a priest receives his support. If so, the nature of the support of a diocesan priest in the United States is "compensation." If not, said support is of the nature of a "gift." [53]

In the United States, under the often misunderstood so-called doctrine of Separation of Church and State,[54] the state has adopted a legal hands off policy regarding the support of the diocesan priests. There is, accordingly, no legislation which provides for any contract implied in law, or more properly called any quasi-contract, in the case of the support of said priests.[55]

There are two types of contract (express or implied) recognized by Canon Law in the United States, as identified with American Law by canon 1529, as providing compensation: (1) a contract involving the status of an employee; and (2) a contract involving the status of an independent contractor.

---

[53]Cf. 26 CFR, Cum. Supp., § 86.8.

[54]For a searching legal analysis of said doctrine consult D. E. O'Brien, "Church and State, Jural Postulates," *Notre Dame Lawyer,* XXIV (1948), 134-140.

[55]In every case reported in any court of record in the United States, without exception, it has been held that no quasi-contractual relationship exists in the case of the support of a diocesan priest from a benefice, office, or subsidy, Mass stipends or stole fees. Cf. *Rose v. Vertin,* 46 Mich. 457 (1881); *Twigg v. Sheehan,* 101 Pa. 363 (1882); *Baxter v. McDonnell,* 155 N. Y. 83 (1898); *Ross v. City of Philadelphia,* 25 Atl. 2d, 834 (1942).

(1) A Contract Involving the Status of an Employee.

A contract of employment results in the legal relationship of master and servant between the master or employer on the one hand, and a servant or employee on the other hand.[56] If a priest receives money as an employee or servant, he would of legal necessity receive it from an employer or master who would have the legal power to discharge him as an employee. "He is deemed to be a master who has the superior choice, control, and direction of the servant, whose will the servant represents not merely in the ultimate result of the work, but in details." [57] "Inasmuch as the right to control involves the power to discharge, the existence of this power is essential, and is an indicium of the relationship." [58]

Generally the relationship of master and servant, or, as it is sometimes called, of employer and employee, exists when the person for whom services are performed has the right to control and to direct the individual who performs the services not only as to the result to be accomplished by the work but also as to the details and means by which that result is accomplished. That is, an employee is subject to the will and control of the employer not only as to what shall be done but as to how it shall be done. In this connection it is not necessary that the employer actually direct or control the manner in which the services are performed; it is sufficient if he has the legal right to do so. The right to discharge is also an important factor in indicating that the person possessing that right is an employer. Other factors characteristic of an employer, but not necessarily present in every case, are the furnishing of tools and the furnishing of a place for work to the individual who performs the services.[59]

(2) A Contract Involving the Status of an Independent Contractor.

An independent contractor is a person who contracts with another to do something for him, but who is not controlled by the other nor subject to the other's right to control with respect to his

[56] 39 C.J., 33.
[57] 39 C.J., 33.
[58] 39 C.J., 35, 36.
[59] 20 CFR, § 402.3.

physical conduct in the performance of any undertaking.[60] In general, if an individual is subject to the control of another merely as to the result to be accomplished by the work, and not as to the means and methods for accomplishing the result, he is an independent contractor. An individual performing services as an independent contractor is not, as to such services, an employee. Generally, physicians, lawyers, dentists, veterinarians, contractors, public stenographers, and others who follow an independent trade, business, or profession in which they offer their services to the public are independent contractors.[61]

If neither of these types of contract at American Canon Law exists expressly or impliedly in the case of diocesan priests as the means whereby they receive their support, then whatever money or bank checks or other goods of value they receive is, by exclusion, of the nature of a "gift." [62]

Article 3. Constituent Elements in the Concept of "Gift"

The concept "gift" is one of the best understood concepts in the entire world. Gifts have been recognized and made part of every system of law from time immemorial.[63] With reference to gifts the Code of Canon Law has adopted the law of the place where a gift is made as the Canon Law of the Church.[64]

---

[60] *Restatement of the Law of Agency* (2 vols., St. Paul: American Law Institute Publishers, 1933), I, § 82 (hereafter cited as *Restatement of Agency).*

[61] 20 CFR, § 402.3. No contention has ever been made in the secular courts of the United States that Catholic priests offer their services to the public for compensation as independent contractors.

[62] Cf. *Bogardus v. Commissioner of Internal Revenue,* 302 U. S. 34 (1937); cf. 26 U. S. C. § 1002.

[63] Cf. Wernz-Vidal, *Ius Canonicum,* IV, II, 332-333; Vermeersch-Creusen, *Epitome,* II, 489-490.

[64] Cf. Vromant, *De Bonis Ecclesiae,* p. 167; Cocchi, *Commentarium,* VI, 421. The Sacred Roman Rota recognizes, gives effect to and applies the law of the place as the Canon Law which regulates the matter of gifts. S. R. R., *Crediti,* 11 iul. 1928, coram R. P. D. Francisco Parrillo, Decisio XXXII—*S.R.R. Dec.* XX (1928), 292-305. The Code of Canon Law does not adopt as Canon Law any territorial law regarding gifts which is contrary to the

A gift at Canon Law in the United States is a voluntary transfer of property by one to another without a legally sufficient consideration.[65] Gifts under the European Canon Law, which likewise follows the civil law of the place, can be and often are subclassified into gifts of various types, all of which are none the less of the nature and the essence of gifts. One such continental subclassification is the remunerative gift.[66]

Although American Canon Law does not generally subclassify gifts, nevertheless there is acknowledged the existence of the subclassification of "remunerative gift"—a gift the purpose of which is voluntarily to recompense for services rendered when there is no obligation, statutory or contractual, so to do.[67] Subclassification of gifts, once the essential nature of a transaction as a gift has been ascertained, is not necessary at American Law—whether Canon or Secular.[68] If in fact it be a gift, that is the end of the matter, and inquiry whether it be a gift of one sort or another is unnecessary and irrelevant at Canon Law in the United States.[69]

Divine Law or to other pertinent provisions of Canon Law itself, whether general or particular. Cf. *supra*, Chapter III, Art. 3, p. 34.

[65]28 C.J., 620; 38 C.J., 779, 780.

[66]Cf. Vermeersch-Creusen, *Epitome*, II, 489-490. A comparison between the European Canon Law and the American Canon Law of the State of Louisiana, which in some respects differs from the Canon Law of the other forty-seven states as to contracts and payments, is of interest, since in Louisiana, which follows a civil law system, gifts are subclassified. Articles 1523 and 1525 of the Compiled Edition of the Civil Codes of Louisiana provide in that state for a subclassification of transactions which are of the nature of a gift, namely that of the "remunerative gift." Cf. K. R. O'Brien, "Foundations for Masses Should Never Create Trusts," *The Jurist*, IV (1944), 284 ff.

[67]Cf. 54 C.J., 377-378. Remuneration here has reference to the motive on account of which the gift is made. As thus used it may be somewhat analogous with the *causa* of the civil law, but it does not indicate any contractual relation with a legally sufficient consideration. Remuneration at Canon Law in the United States can accordingly be either the result of a contract and thereby be contractual compensation, or it can be a voluntary gift. 51 C.J., 124. This indicates that words may not be univocal even within the same system of law.

[68]*Bogardus v. Commissioner of Internal Revenue*, 302 U. S. 34.

[69]*Supra*, p. 50.

The essential elements of a gift at Canon Law in the United States require that:

1. There must be a donor.[70]

2. The donor must be competent to make a gift, i.e., he must have legal capacity.[71]

3. The donor must have an intention to make a gift, i.e., a voluntary transfer of property to another without a legally sufficient consideration. Unless the donor intends to make a voluntary transfer, no gift is possible. There can be no intention to make a gift if the transferor of property intends to receive a legally sufficient consideration for the transfer.[72] To be voluntary at Canon Law in the United States a transfer of property must not be in satisfaction of any contractual obligation.[73] The motive for making a gift is not material.[74] The intention of the parties controls in determining whether a payment is in fact a gift or compensation. The fact that the recipient is not an employee is at times persuasive that the payment is a gift. If no (temporal) services have been rendered at any time, the payments may well constitute gifts.[75]

4. There must be a delivery of the subject matter of the gift.[76] Delivery need not be made directly to the donee.[77] Delivery to a third party in behalf of the donee is enough.[78] The fact that the amount of the gift received by a diocesan priest may be specified by his bishop does not affect the essential elements of the transaction. Liberty of specification, by which the amount of a gift is

---

[70] *Edson v. Lucas,* 40 F. 2d 398.

[71] *Willis v. Garey,* 16 B.T.A. 274.

[72] *Helvering v. American Dental Co.,* 318 U. S. 322; *Merrill v. Fahs,* 324 U. S. 308; 26 U. S. C. § 1002.

[73] *Lester v. U. S.,* 35 Fed. Supp. 535, stands for the position that when a transfer is made in satisfaction of any contractual obligation it is not to be classified as a gift but as contractual compensation.

[74] Mertens, *Taxation,* I, § 6.08. Cf. O'Brien and O'Brien, "How New York Restricts Gifts for Masses," *Fordham Law Review,* XIII (1944), 175 ff., at pp. 187-190.

[75] Mertens, *Taxation,* I, § 8.08.

[76] *Larson,* B.T.A. Memo. Jan. 17, 1940, aff'd 117 F. 2d 821.

[77] *Richardson v. Commissioner,* 126 F. 2d 562.

[78] *City Bank Farmers Trust Co. v. Hoey,* 23 Fed. Supp. 831, aff'd 101 F. 2d 9.

determined, is not of the essence, but, as Merkelbach (1871-1942) stated, is a "perfection" of liberty.[79] The faculty of choosing between contradictories, or between giving and not giving is the only element of essence in a voluntary transfer.[80]

5. There must be an absence of any legal consideration.[81] A gift is a gratuity, an act of generosity, and not only does not require a consideration, but necessarily precludes a consideration. If there is a legally sufficient consideration for the transaction, then the transaction denotes not a gift but a contractual compensation.[82] The absence of a consideration is not necessarily the same as the lack of a *quid pro quo*.[83] All surrounding circumstances are relevant.[84]

6. There must be a donee competent to accept the gift.[85]

7. The donee must accept the gift.[86]

For the purposes of this study it is sufficient to note that, if a transfer of property by one to another be the result of a contract, it is of the nature of contractual compensation, and if there be no contract, it is at Canon Law in the United States of the nature of a gift.[87] When there is no contractual relation between the parties, nor any contractual obligation on the part of the payor to the recipient, payments constitute gifts.[88]

A determination of the nature of support of diocesan priests in the United States resolves itself into the simple question: Is there

---

[79] *Summa Theologiae Moralis* (3 ed., 3 vols., Parisiis: Typis Desclée de Brouwer et Soc., 1938-1939), I, 87.

[80] Cf. K. O'Brien, "The Priest and the Victory Tax—Replication," *The Jurist*, III (1943), 452 ff.

[81] 26 U.S.C., § 1002; 26 CFR, Cum. Supp., § 86.8; *Botchford v. Commissioner*, 81 F. 2d 914; *Combs v. Roark's Adm'r*, 221 Ky. 679, 229 S.W. 576.

[82] 38 C.J., 337-338; 28 C.J., 620.

[83] *Weagant v. Bowers*, 57 F. 2d 697.

[84] *Schall v. Commissioner of Internal Revenue*, 11 T. C. No. 16.

[85] R. Montgomery, *Montgomery's Federal Taxes* (1947-1948 edition, New York: The Ronald Press Co., 1948), p. 895.

[86] *Montgomery's Federal Taxes*, 895.

[87] *Bogardus v. Commissioner of Internal Revenue*, 302 U. S. 34 (1937), as read in connection with canon 1529.

[88] *Weagant v. Bowers*, 57 F. 2d 679 (1932); Mertens, *Taxation*, I, § 8.08.

at American Canon Law a contract under which the priest receives his support? If there is a contract, then the support received by a diocesan priest in the United States is of the nature of compensation. If there is no contract, then the support received by a diocesan priest in the United States is of the nature of a gift. To determine the answer to the question regarding the nature of the support of diocesan priests in the United States one turns to the law of the Church, primarily the Code of Canon Law, secondarily the law of the Plenary Councils of Baltimore.[89]

[89]It should be noted that the nature of support of diocesan priests may differ in the United States from the nature of this support in various European countries. As Pound says, a sale is a sale at Amsterdam and at New York. Yet the legal understanding and treatment of the transaction in the two places may be very different. Cf. *HLR,* XLVII (1933), 1 at 11; *supra,* pp. 23-24. Pistocchi *(De Re Beneficiali,* p. 410) indicates the same point when he asserts that the nature of support of a beneficiary in Italy is determined under Articles 477, 511, and 481 of the Italian Civil Code, while in France it is determined under Art. IV of the French Statutes. Pistocchi asserts that there is an analogy between the support of a beneficiary in Italy and that of a usufructuary, while in France this support is of the juridic nature of that of a stipendiary, and in Austria it is expressly by the law of the place declared to be of the nature of a usufruct. The European concept of usufruct and usufructuary is not found as such in the American Law, and although the transaction may be similar, it is understood and treated differently under American Law. Since the American Law has been adopted by the Code of Canon Law as the Canon Law on contracts and payments, the Canon Law treatment of the nature of the transaction will in the United States be necessarily understood and applied differently than in other countries.

Chapter V

THE NATURE OF SUPPORT OF DIOCESAN PRIESTS FROM A BENEFICE

Article 1. Preliminary Notions

The Ordinary must confer upon each priest whom he promotes on the title of service of the diocese *a benefice,* an office, or a subsidy sufficient for his adequate support.[1] The Code of Canon Law defines an ecclesiastical benefice as a juridic entity permanently constituted or erected by competent ecclesiastical authority, consisting of a sacred office, and furnishing the right to receive revenue from the endowment connected with the office.[2] Four requirements are necessary for the constituting of an ecclesiastical benefice: a sacred office, the right to receive revenue from the endowment connected with the office, the erection of the benefice as a juridic entity, and, finally, perpetual continuity.[3] The authors distinguish in every benefice: the office, the right to the revenue and the revenue itself. The office is something spiritual, the right to the revenue is something annexed to the spiritual, and the revenue is something temporal.[4]

At the present time in the United States practically the only existing benefices are parishes. Every canonically established parish

[1]Canon 981, § 2 (translation by the writer, italics inserted); cf. Vermeersch-Creusen, *Epitome,* II, 143.

[2]Canon 1409; cf. Vermeersch-Creusen, *Epitome,* II, 431; De Meester, *Compendium,* III, I, 321; Pistocchi, *De Re Beneficiali,* pp. 5-16.

[3]A. Cance, *Le Code de Droit Canonique* (12 ed., 3 vols., Paris: Gabalda et Fils, 1929), III, 185-186 (hereafter cited as *Le Code*); M. Coronata, *Institutiones Iuris Canonici* (2 ed., 5 vols., Taurini: Marietti, 1939-1947), II, 357-358 (hereafter cited as *Institutiones*); De Meester, *Compendium,* III, I, 321-322; Pistocchi, *De Re Beneficiali,* pp. 9-14.

[4]Cf. canon 1413, § 2; Coronata, *Institutiones,* II, 357-358; Vermeersch-Creusen, *Epitome,* II, 431; De Meester, *Compendium,* III, I, 322-326; Pistocchi, *De Re Beneficiali,* p. 14.

in the United States constitutes a benefice.[5] From the very nature of the parochial office and from the position of being entrusted with the care of souls for their eternal welfare, the pastor of a parish has certain definite and grave obligations. As a priest who holds a sacred office he is responsible to God for aiding the congregation in the discharge of their spiritual obligations. Men are bound to acknowledge God as their supreme Lord and first beginning, and to strive toward Him as their last end. They always have felt the need of having the service of a priesthood rendered unto them. According to the definition given by St. Paul, the priest and pastor is a man "taken from amongst men," yet "ordained for men in the things that appertain to God." His office is not established for the temporal interests of human beings and for the things that pass away, however lofty and valuable these may seem, but for things divine and enduring in the plan of the redemption of the human race.[6] The pastor of the parish is the priest who holds this sacred office, and as such he has the right to receive the revenue from the endowment attached to that office.[7]

The endowment of the benefices in the United States normally consists of the voluntary offerings of the faithful.[8] These offerings are divided into two parts, the first yielding to the church, the second being assigned to the pastor for his support.[9] The amount of the portion set apart for the pastor is determined by the bishop,

[5]Pontifical Commission for the Authentic Interpretation of the Canons of the Code, reply of Sept. 26, 1921, Cf. Bouscaren, *The Canon Law Digest*, I, 149-151, under canon 216; W. Allen, *De Existentia Beneficiorum Paroecialium ante et post Codicem in Statibus Foederatis Americae* (Rome: Anonima Libreria Cattolica Italiana, 1938), pp. 83-87 (hereafter cited as *Existentia Beneficiorum).*

[6]Cf. Pius XI, litt. encycl. *"Ad Catholici sacerdotii,"* 20 dec. 1935—*AAS*, XXVIII (1936) 5-53 (Vatican Press Translation).

[7]Canon 451, § 1. Cf. canons 979 and 981, § 2; cf. also Vermeersch-Creusen, *Epitome*, II, 277 ff.; Blat, *Commentarium* II, 483.

[8]Cf. canons 1410; 1415, § 1; 1415, § 3; Vermeersch-Creusen, *Epitome*, II, 432; De Meester, *Compendium*, III, I, 322-323 and 327; Coronata, *Institutiones*, II, 361, 366; Pistocchi, *De Re Beneficiali*, pp. 21-22; Allen, *Existentia Beneficiorum*, p. 110.

[9]Allen, *Existentia Beneficiorum*, p. 110.

and is called the priest's *congrua* or salary.[10] If this amount is more than is *de facto* needed by the priest for his adequate support, he must utilize the superfluous amount for the poor or other pious causes, for it is assigned to him *ad sustentandum eum, non ditandum.*[11] It has well been stated that although the voluntary offerings of the faithful are not paid directly to the pastor, it remains true that the fund from which his support comes is made up of the voluntary contributions of the faithful, a portion of which the diocesan authority applies for his support.[12] This voluntary support, put into practice in the United States by the Synod of 1791, was reaffirmed in an Instruction issued by the Sacred Congregation of the Propagation of the Faith on May 13, 1816, to the effect that the diocesan priests in the United States should receive their support from the voluntary contributions of the faithful.[13]

A diocesan priest is appointed to a benefice by the ordinary of the place in which the benefice is located.[14] In a few instances, however, the appointment to a benefice may come to a diocesan priest directly from the Holy See.[15] No one, in any case, can ever confer a benefice upon himself.[16] The appointment of a priest to

---

[10]III Plenary Council of Baltimore, Decree 273. Salary is used in this connection with a technical canonical meaning which differs from its technical meaning at American Secular Law. Cf. *supra,* p. 18.

[11]Canon 1473; cf. Allen, "The Parish-Benefice Revenue," *The Jurist,* VIII (1948), 323 ff. It may here be noted that this obligation has been denied by certain writers for priests in the United States. Certainly money from non-ecclesiastical sources is not to be included in calculations of superfluous support. Allen, *Existentia Beneficiorum,* p. 111.

[12]Hannan, "The Cleric's Last Will," *The Jurist,* VIII (1948), 59-60; cf. 1791 Synod, Statute VII, *supra* p. 12, *Coll. Lac.* III, 3.

[13]S.C. de Prop. Fide, 13 maii 1816, ad 2—*Collectanea,* n. 713; Fontes, n. 4705.

[14]Canon 1432, § 1. Cf. Cance, *Le Code,* III, 191; Coronata, *Institutiones,* II, 387; Vermeersch-Creusen, *Epitome,* II, 443-444; De Meester, *Compendium,* III, I, 340-341; Pistocchi, *De Re Beneficiali,* p. 166.

[15]Cf. canon 1435; Cance, *Le Code,* III, 191; Coronata, *Institutiones,* II, 383; Vermeersch-Creusen, *Epitome,* II, 444; De Meester, *Compendium,* III, I, 341; Pistocchi, *De Re Beneficiali,* pp. 186-187.

[16]Canon 1437; De Meester, *Compendium* III, I, 342; Cance, *Le Code,* III, 192; Vermeersch-Creusen, *Epitome,* II, 444; Coronata, *Institutiones,* II, 391.

a secular benefice is ordinarily made for the lifetime of the appointee.[17]

After receiving his appointment to a benefice, a secular priest must take canonical possession of the benefice by what is called a *missio in possessionem,* or a corporal institution. This *missio in possessionem* is under the direction and control of the ordinary of the place.[18] If a priest after being appointed to a benefice, but before taking canonical possession thereof, attempts either to take possession himself without a *missio in possessionem* from the ordinary or to interfere in the administration of the benefice he becomes automatically ineligible for the benefice and is subject to punishment by the ordinary.[19]

From the moment of taking legitimate canonical possession of his benefice, the beneficiary enjoys all the rights, both spiritual and temporal, connected at Canon Law with his benefice.[20] Even though the beneficiary has other funds which did not derive from his benefice, he may freely use any fruits of his benefice that may be necessary for his adequate support. Any amount in excess of what is needed for his support must, however, be utilized for the poor or for pious causes.[21]

---

[17]Canon 1438; Coronata, *Institutiones,* II, 388; Cance, *Le Code,* III, 192; De Meester, *Compendium,* III, I, 342-343; Vermeersch-Creusen, *Epitome,* II, 446; Pistocchi, *De Re Beneficiali,* pp. 202-203.

[18]Canons 1443-1444; Pistocchi, *De Re Beneficiali,* p. 227; Vermeersch-Creusen, *Epitome,* II, 447-448; Cance, *Le Code,* III, 192; Coronata, *Institutiones,* II, 391; De Meester, *Compendium,* III, I, 343-344.

[19]Canon 2394; De Meester, *Compendium,* III, II, 285; Vermeersch-Creusen, *Epitome,* III, 378; Coronata, *Institutiones,* IV, 670; Pistocchi, *De Re Beneficiali,* p. 223; Blat, *Commentarium,* VI, 309-310.

[20]Canon 1472; Cance, *Le Code,* III, 194; Coronata, *Institutiones,* II, 414; Vermeersch-Creusen, *Epitome,* II, 457; De Meester, *Compendium,* III, I, 347; Pistocchi, *De Re Beneficiali,* pp. 409-410.

[21]Regarding beneficiaries in the United States there has been some discussion relative to this obligation. Cf. Hannan, "The Clerics Last Will," *The Jurist,* VIII (1948), 41 ff.; and Allen, "The Parish-Benefice Revenue," *The Jurist,* VIII (1948), 323 ff. Cf. canon 1473; Pistocchi, *De Re Beneficiali,* pp. 411-420; Allen, *Existentia Beneficiorum,* pp. 110-111; Coronata, *Institutiones,* II, 414; Cance, *Le Code,* III, 194; Vermeersch-Creusen, *Epitome,* II, 457-458; De Meester, *Compendium,* III, I, 347-348.

The whole law touching benefices was reorganized in the Code of Canon Law. This is definitely stated in a decision of the Sacred Congregation of the Council.[22] Old laws respecting benefices are therefore without present juridical force. Hence old commentaries on the laws of Boniface VIII (1294-1303) and Benedict XIV (1740-1758), as also the statements of certain decretalists, are to be read with circumspection and with an eye to canon 6, 6°, which states that any disciplinary laws which were in effect prior to the Code of Canon Law but which are neither explicitly nor implicitly contained in the Code are by that very fact to be regarded as having lost all force.[23]

After the Divine Law, the Code of Canon Law occupies the first place in the current legislation of the Church. The I Provincial Council of Baltimore indicated in 1791 that the Divine Law provided for support of priests by the voluntary contributions of the faithful.[24] Once conceding that the Divine Law provided for the nature of support of priests, and postulating that the Divine Law is immutable, it follows that the Code of Canon Law would not contain any provision which would purport to change the Divine Law with regard to the nature of support of diocesan priests.[25]

The determination of the nature of support received by a diocesan priest in the United States from a benefice at the present time presents the question: Is there at Canon Law, as identified with American Law,[26] a legally enforceable contract under which the priest receives his support from a benefice? If there is such a contract at Canon Law, then the support received by a priest from his benefice is of the nature of "compensation." If there is no such contract, then the support received by a priest from a benefice is of the nature of a "gift."[27]

---

[22] *AAS,* XXXII (1940), 377.

[23] E. Roelker, "The Right to Revenue During Non-Residence," *The Jurist,* I (1941), 76.

[24] Statute 23, *Coll. Lac.,* III, 6.

[25] Cf. Blat, *Commentarium,* III, 410; Vermeersch-Creusen, *Epitome,* II, 143-144.

[26] Canon 1529. Cf. the manner in which Pistocchi in his work *De Re Beneficiali* utilizes Italian, French, and Austrian law in determining the nature of the support from a benefice in those countries.

[27] *Supra,* chapters III and IV.

It has been suggested that there is the execution of a contract, or at least an implied contract, at Canon Law in the accepting of a benefice. The beneficiary assertedly agrees to certain conditions which must be scrupulously fulfilled if the fruits of his benefice are to accrue to him.[28] It has been suggested on the other hand that there is no contract whatsoever, either express or implied, whether in fact or in law, at *Canon Law in the United States,* whereby a priest receives support from a benefice.[29]

Article 2. Is the Diocesan Priest Supported from a Benefice by Reason of a Contract?

There are at least three fundamental tests as to whether there is at Canon Law in the United States a legally enforceable contract[30] whereby a priest receives his support from a benefice. The non-existence of any one of these three will preclude the possibility of the existence of a contract:[31]

(1) The right to discharge the priest from his benefice.[32]

(2) The right to control the priest in the details of his priestly work.[33]

(3) The existence of a legally sufficient consideration to bring a contract into being.[34]

Sec. 1. The Right to Discharge the Priest from his Benefice

The existence of the legal power to discharge is essential to the

[28] E. Roelker, "The Right to Revenue During Non-Residence," *The Jurist,* I (1941), 76; M. Lennon, "The Priest and the Victory Tax: Another View," *The Jurist,* III (1943), 441. In *O'Callaghan v. O'Sullivan,* [1925] 1 Ir. R. 90, it was suggested by way of a mere *obiter dictum* that the legal relationship of a pastor with his bishop was contractual in character.

[29] K. O'Brien, "The Priest and the Victory Tax—Replication," *The Jurist,* III (1943), 455. Compare the decision that in the Scotch Episcopal Church there is no contract relationship in a benefice. *Brook v. Kelly* [1893] A. C. 721.

[30] Cf. Williston, *Contracts,* I, §§ 233-241, esp. § 241; §§ 20-60, esp. § 37; § 72.

[31] 39 C.J., 35.

[32] Cf. 39 C.J., 35, 36.

[33] Cf. 39 C.J., 33.

[34] *Restatement of Contracts,* § 19 and § 75 ff.

existence of a contract of employment. The power to discharge a priest from a benefice would be an indicium of the existence of such a contract whereby the priest receives his support from the benefice.[35] In the United States practically the only benefices conferred upon diocesan priests are parishes.[36] Although normally each parish benefice is conferred upon the diocesan priest for the duration of his life, he may cease to hold the benefice through resignation, deprivation, removal, transfer, or the lapse of the term of appointment.[37] It is to be noted that there is no provision in the Code of Canon Law which gives to any one the power to discharge a priest from his benefice in the manner in which an employee can be discharged by his employer—with an immediate and perpetual loss of any right to further monetary support.[38]

Although a diocesan priest may resign his benefice, it is not permitted to the ordinary to accept such a resignation unless there be a just and a proportionate reason therefor.[39] Not only is the ordinary not permitted to accept the resignation without a just and proportionate reason, but in addition the ordinary is not permitted to accept the resignation of a benefice by a priest unless it is certain that the priest has all things necessary for his adequate support from some other source.[40]

---

[35]Cf. 39 C.J., 35, 36.

[36]Cf. *supra*, p. 57. To some diocesan priests, however, the Pope confers consistorial benefices, namely, when he appoints them as residential bishops. The legal nature of the support of residential bishops is identical with that of pastors, since both receive their support from a benefice.

[37]Canon 183, § 1. This is an exhausive enumeration. Cf. Coronata, *Institutiones*, I, 279; Wernz-Vidal, *Ius Canonicum*, II, 387; J. Brys, *Juris Canonici Compendium* (Brugis: Desclée de Brouwer et Sii, 1947), pp. 265 sqq. (hereafter cited as *Compendium*); Blat, *Commentarium*, II, 155-156.

[38]Cf. 39 C.J., 35, 36; canons 1484, 2162, 2163, 2154, 2303, 2304.

[39]Canons 184, 189, § 1; Brys, *Compendium*, pp. 266-267; Vermeersch-Creusen, *Epitome*, I, 172-173; Blat, *Commentarium*, II, 155-156, 159; Pistocchi, *De Re Beneficiali*, p. 475; G. McDevitt, *The Renunciation of an Ecclesiastical Office*, The Catholic University of America Canon Law Studies, n. 218 (Washington, D. C.: The Catholic University of America Press, 1946), p. 62 (hereafter cited as *Renunciation)*.

[40]Canon 1484. Such a source may well exist under canon 979, § 2, in the office or subsidy required by this canon to be conferred upon the priest by the ordinary, or in an ecclesiastical pension conferred under canon 1429, § 2.

When the incumbent resigns his benefice he is not discharged from it, but rather he voluntarily relinquishes his incumbency. Even if the beneficiary wishes to resign, the ordinary cannot licitly accept the resignation for which the Code gives its warrant unless he is assured that the priest has other means of decent support. Proof to this effect must be given before the ordinary can lawfully accept the resignation, which in effect means that at times the ordinary is charged with actually requiring the priest to retain his benefice. The fact that a resignation is permitted under the Code does not imply the power or the authority of the ordinary to discharge a priest from his incumbency.[41]

In the case of the transfer of a priest from a benefice there must be at the same time the conferral upon the priest of another benefice of approximately equal rank.[42] This procedure is not the same thing as a discharge from an office whereby all rights to support cease, as is the case in which support is granted through a contract of employment.[43]

The Code of Canon Law provides several processes, penal and non-penal, administrative and judicial, for the removal of a priest from his benefice. This is a different concept from that of the discharge of an employee from his employment in such a manner that he no longer has any legal claim to receive money or support.[44] In the case of a non-penal administrative removal of a priest from his benefice the bishop is required either to transfer the priest to another benefice, or to assign another office to him if he be capable

---

Cf. Vermeersch-Creusen, *Epitome,* II, 461; De Meester, *Compendium,* III, I, 352; Pistocchi, *De Re Beneficiali,* pp. 477-478; McDevitt, *Renunciation,* pp. 65-66.

[41]Under no circumstances whatsoever is a priest permitted to resign his benefice into the hands of the laity. To tender a resignation to any member of the laity subjects the priest to a severe penalty. Cf. canon 2400; Pistocchi, *De Re Beneficiali,* p. 474.

[42]Cf. canons 2162, 2163. Cappello, *Summa,* III, 381; Coronata, *Institutiones,* III, 528-530; Vermeersch-Creusen, *Epitome,* III, 202-203.

[43]Cf. 39 C.J., 35, 36.

[44]*In re Public Ledger,* 63 F. Supp. 1008. Cf. canons 2147, 2182, 2154; cf. also Cappello, *Summa,* III, 376; Coronata, *Institutiones,* III, 522-524; Vermeersch-Creusen, *Epitome,* III, 199-200.

of receiving it, or to confer upon the priest a pension, or a subsidy, as the circumstances of the particular case may warrant.[45]

In addition to the non-penal administrative removal from office, the Code of Canon Law provides[46] for both an administrative and a judicial penal removal from or deprivation of office with reference to priests who have culpably and seriously violated specific canons. Under his title of ordination a diocesan priest has a right to look for support to his ordinary, who has the correlative duty to confer upon him what suffices for his adequate support.[47] This right is not lost to the priest through either an administrative or a judicial penal removal from office.[48]

In two cases only is a bishop authorized under the Code of Canon Law so to dismiss a priest from a benefice that the priest is no longer entitled to receive support. These cases involve the deposition of a man from the priesthood and the privation of the right ever to wear the ecclesiastical garb.[49] In both these cases the man ceases to function as a priest. But even though a priest be deposed from the priesthood for a cause, it is nonetheless required that the bishop, through his charity, in whatever manner he may see fit, shall provide support to that priest, lest the latter be forced to beg with shame and disgrace to the clerical state. This obligation on the part of the bishop is, as was just noted, one of charity only, and not one of legal justice. It is not enforceable in any way at Canon Law.[49a] If the man does not show some signs of emenda-

[45]Canon 2154; cf. Vermeersch-Creusen, *Epitome,* III, 199-200; Coronata, *Institutiones,* III, 522-524.

[46]Canons 2396; 2266; 2314; 2177, 3°; 2180; 2181; 2359, § 1; 2331, § 2; 2354, § 2; 2340, § 2; 2343, § 2, 3°; 2359, § 2, 3; 2368, § 1; 2345; 2346; 2350, § 2; 2381, § 2; 2360, § 2; 2355; 2405, 2394, 2°; 2403; 2336, § 2; 2359 § 3; 2401.

[47]Cf. Canon 981 § 2; Vermeersch-Creusen, *Epitome,* II, 143.

[48]Schmalzgrueber, *Jus Ecclesiasticum,* Lib. V., tit. 39, n. 305; III Plenary Council of Baltimore, Decree n. 72; S. C. de Prop. Fide, 4 febr. 1873, ad 1—*Collectanea,* n. 1394; Fontes, n. 4881; *infra,* pp. 99-100.

[49]Canons 2304 and 2303; cf. Vermeersch-Creusen, *Epitome,* III, 302-305; Coronata, *Institutiones,* IV, 270-277.

[49a]Canon 2302, § 2; cf. Coronata, *Institutiones,* IV, 270-276; Vermeersch-Creusen, *Epitome,* III, 301-305.

tion of life, but continues to give scandal by his mode of living, then the bishop may, by decree, deprive him perpetually of the right of wearing the ecclesiastical garb. This privation brings with it the loss even of receiving any charitable provision for support.[49b]

It has already been noted that the Sacred Congregation for the Propagation of the Faith in a response, on February 4, 1873, to the Bishop of Natchez, although that diocese was admittedly one of the poorest of the dioceses of the United States at the time, required the diocese to provide decent support to a diocesan priest who through his own fault had become unworthy of serving any congregation. The response declared that the bishop could not refuse to give the priest decent support even though his removal from his parish had been justified, unless, after repeated warnings, the priest did not amend his life and thus manifested contumacy.[49c]

There is, accordingly, no right on the part of the bishop, or of any other person, to discharge a priest from his benefice to the extent that the priest ceases to have a right to receive fitting support so long as the priest has not been deprived by penal judicial process of the right to support as flowing from his title of ordination. Removal from a benefice, whether administrative or judicial, penal or non-penal, does not of itself deprive a priest of the right to support flowing from his title of ordination for the service of the diocese. This is quite a different concept from that of discharge, as that concept is used in connection with a contract of employment. It follows that there is no contract of employment in the case of a diocesan priest who receives his support from a benefice; there is lacking one of the essential elements of a contract of employment.

Sec. 2. The Right to Control the Priest as to the Details of his Priestly Work

When the person for whom services are performed has the right at law to control and direct the individual who performs the services not only as to the result to be accomplished but also as to the

[49b]Canon 2304; cf. Vermeersch-Creusen, *Epitome,* III, 301-305; Coronata, *Institutiones,* IV, 270-276.

[49c]*Collectanea,* n. 1394; *Fontes,* n. 4881.

details and means by which that result is accomplished there is ordinarily a contract of employment. In this connection it is not necessary that the employer actually direct or control the manner in which services are performed. It is sufficient that he has the right to do so.[50]

At the time of his ordination to the priesthood each diocesan priest promises obedience to his bishop, and to the latter's successors in office.[51] In addition to this personal promise of obedience, the Code of Canon Law states that every priest is bound by a special obligation to show obedience to his ordinary.[52] However, the scope of this obedience is limited by the Code of Canon Law to the acceptance and the fulfillment, in accordance with the norms of the Code, of any duty imposed upon the priest by the ordinary to satisfy the needs of the Church.[53]

In the case of a beneficiary, the ordinary has under Canon Law the right and duty of supervision and vigilance to see to it that the priest shall administer the affairs of the benefice in accordance with the prescriptions of the Code of Canon Law. But the power of the ordinary to issue specific instructions as to the administration of the details of a benefice is expressly limited, so that the ordinary's jurisdiction can be exercised only within the limits of the Code of Canon Law.[54]

This limited power of supervision flows from the fundamental canon that the ordinary has the right and duty of governing his diocese only *ad normam sacrorum canonum.*[55] This restriction on

---

[50]Cf. 39 C.J., 33; 20 CFR, Cum. Suppl. § 404.104.

[51]Cf. Rite of Ordination; cf. Vermeersch-Creusen, *Epitome,* I, 143.

[52]Canon 127; cf. Brys, *Compendium,* pp. 224-226; Cappello, *Summa,* I, 200.

[53]Canon 128; cf. canons 335, § 2, and 336, § 1; Brys, *Compendium,* pp. 225-226; Cappello, *Summa,* I, 329-332.

[54]Canon 1519; cf. canon 336, § 1; De Meester, *Compendium,* III, I, 394-395; Cappello, *Summa,* III, 570-571; Vermeersch-Creusen, *Epitome,* I, 242-243. Beyond the ruling of the Code the ordinary may enjoy certain faculties and privileges as extended to him by the Roman Pontiff. The tenor of these can be ascertained only by an examination of the rescript in each particular case.

[55]Canon 335, § 1; Cappello, *Summa* I, 329-332; Vermeersch-Creusen, *Epitome,* I, 242-244; Blat, *Commentarium,* II, 350-351; G. Ryan, *Principles*

the power and the authority of the ordinary is such that he is obliged to enforce the observance of the ecclesiastical laws, and is restrained from dispensing from them except in those cases in which the power to dispense is expressly given him.[56]

The power of the ordinary is limited to vigilance lest abuses creep into the ecclesiastical discipline, especially with regard to the administration of the sacraments and sacramentals, the worship of God and the honor of the Saints, and the preaching of the word of God. The ordinary is required to see to it that the purity of faith is preserved in both the clergy and the people, that the faithful receive adequate instruction in the truths of Christian doctrine, and that the children be given the opportunity of a Catholic education in the schools.[57]

Although there is vested in the ordinary this extensive power of vigilance and supervision regarding the aims and purposes to be achieved, a search of the Code of Canon Law fails to show that the ordinary legally has the direct power of detailed administration over the benefice held by a diocesan priest, or over the detailed activities of the priest in administering his benefice.[58] The duties of the priest beneficiary are clearly set forth in the Code of Canon Law itself as resting upon the priest personally.[59] The performance of these duties in their various details is imposed by the Code of Canon Law and does not depend upon any mutual promises, or even unilateral promise, made between the priest and the bishop.[60]

It follows that the bishop does not, by contract, have the right to control directly the details of the priestly work of a beneficiary in the administration of his benefice. Since this essential indicium

---

of Episcopal Jurisdiction, The Catholic University of America Canon Law Studies, n. 120 (Washington, D. C.: The Catholic University of America Press, 1939) pp. 133-135 (hereafter cited as *Episcopal Jurisdiction).*

[56]Canon 336, § 1; Cappello, *Summa*, I, 329-332; Blat, *Commentarium*, II, 351-353.

[57]Canon 336, § 2.

[58]Cf. Comyns, *Administration*, p. 135; Ryan, *Episcopal Jurisdiction*, pp. 133-135.

[59]As examples, not all-inclusive however, cf. canons 461, 462, 464, 465, 466, 467, 468, 470, 1472-1483.

[60]Cf. canons 12, 13.

is missing, it further follows that there is no contract of employment whereby a diocesan priest receives his support from a benefice.

Sec. 3. The Existence of a Legally Sufficient Consideration to Bring a Contract into Being

A legally sufficient consideration is essential to the existence at Canon Law in the United States of every contract.[61] Every ecclesiastical benefice is at the same time an ecclesiastical office in the strict sense.[62] Since each benefice is at the same time an ecclesiastical office, the conclusion as to the existence or the non-existence of a legally sufficient consideration to bring a contract into being is the same with regard to the support received from a benefice and the support received from an office. This point will be treated at length in Chapter VI, Article 2, Section 3, p. 80, *infra,* at which point it will be demonstrated that at Canon Law in the United States there is no legally sufficient consideration, since the priest receives his support from the voluntary offerings of the faithful, who are obliged simply in conscience to provide a sufficient support for the priest, and not because of any contractual relationship entitling the priest to support.[63]

Article 3. Is the Support of a Diocesan Priest from a Benefice of the Nature of a "Gift"?

The support received by a diocesan priest from his benefice comes from the voluntary contributions of the faithful. From the moment he takes legitimate possession of his benefice a beneficiary is permitted freely to use the funds contributed by the faithful for

---

[61]Cf. canon 1529; *supra,* chapter IV; Vermeersch-Creusen, *Epitome,* II, 485-486.

[62]Cf. canon 1409; cf. Pistocchi, *De Re Beneficiali,* pp. 11-13; De Meester, *Compendium,* III, I, 322; Cappello, *Summa,* II, 509-510.

[63]Cf. *Tuigg v. Sheehan,* 101 Pa. 363 (1882); S. C. de Prop. Fide, 13 maii 1816, *Collectanea,* n. 713; *Fontes,* n. 4705; also cf. Williston, *Contracts,* I, §§ 111, 147.

his adequate support, but no more than is necessary should be so used.[64]

There is no contractual relationship at Canon Law in the United States under which the priest receives this support.[65] When assigned by his bishop to a parish as beneficiary, the diocesan priest does not enter into any contract, whether express or implied, with the parishioners or the bishop.[66] When there is no contractual relation between the parties payments constitute gifts.[67] By a process of elimination, then, it follows that the support received by a diocesan priest in the United States from a benefice, since it is not of a contractual nature or a compensation, is of the nature of a "gift."[68]

---

[64]*Collectanea,* n. 713; *Fontes,* n. 4705; canon 1473; Cance, *Le Code,* III, 194; Coronata, *Institutiones,* II, 414; Vermeersch-Creusen, *Epitome,* II, 457-458; De Meester *Compendium,* III, I, 347-348; Capello, *Summa,* II, 535; Pistocchi, *De Re Beneficiali,* pp. 412-420; Vromant, *De Bonis Ecclesiae,* p. 229.

[65]Cf. *supra,* pp. 62 ff.

[66]Cf. *supra,* pp. 62-69; *infra,* pp. 82 sqq.

[67]*Weagant v. Bowers,* 57 F. 2d 679 (1932) ; Mertens, *Taxation,* I, § 8.08. Note that "a gift may be of a right to money for a period of time with a reservation of remainder in the property itself."—*Montgomery's Federal Taxes,* 889.

[68]Cf. *Bogardus v. Commissioner of Internal Revenue,* 302 U. S. 34 (1937). Cf. *supra,* pp. 48-50.

CHAPTER VI

THE NATURE OF SUPPORT OF DIOCESAN PRIESTS FROM AN OFFICE

ARTICLE 1. PRELIMINARY NOTIONS

The ordinary must confer upon each priest whom he promotes on the title of service of the diocese a benefice, or *an office,* or a subsidy, sufficient for his adequate support.[1] An ecclesiastical office, in the wide sense, is any commission which is entrusted to someone to be legitimately exercised for a spiritual end. In the strict sense, an ecclesiastical office is a position which is firmly established either by divine or ecclesiastical ordinance, which is to be conferred according to the norms of the sacred canons, and which carries with it at least some participation in ecclesiastical power, whether of orders or of jurisdiction.[2] An ecclesiastical office at Canon Law differs from and is not the same as a public office at American Secular Law, the holding of which is forbidden by canon 139, § 2, to clerics apart from their possession of an apostolic indult. An ecclesisatical office also differs from a private office in secular corporations and other business concerns, the holding of which is forbidden to diocesan priests by canon 142, and penalized under canon 2830.[3] It has been suggested that the posi-

[1]Canon 981, § 2 [translation by the writer; italics inserted]; cf. Vermeersch-Creusen, *Epitome,* II, 147; Sipos, *Enchiridion,* p. 447.

[2]Canon 145, § 1; Coronata, *Institutiones,* I, 239-240; A. Toso, *Ad Codicem Juris Canonici . . . Commentaria Minora* (5 vols. in 2, Taurini: Marietti, 1918-1927), II, 111-112 (hereafter cited as *Commentaria).*

[3]Cf. J. Brunini, *The Clerical Obligations of Canons 139 and 142,* The Catholic University of America Canon Law Studies, n. 103 (Washington, D. C.: The Catholic University of America, 1937) pp. 20-23; 76 (hereafter cited *Clerical Obligations*); cf. II Plenary Council of Baltimore, Decree 157; III Plenary Council of Baltimore, Decree 82; cf. also R. Pound, "A Comparison of the Ideals of Law," *HLR,* XLVII (1933), 1. In treating the nature of support of diocesan priests, it is the opinion of the writer that

tion of a priest in the United States is analogous to that of officers of social, literary, fraternal, athletic, and similar organizations.[4] But this assertion "is not sound."[5] Moreover, an ecclesiastical office differs from an office in the military establishment of the secular government.[6]

The distinction between an ecclesiastical office and an ecclesiastical benefice is to be kept in mind. An office is very much like the genus, and as such is divided into two species: an office which is at the same time a benefice, and an office which is not at the same time a benefice.[7] In the present legislation of the Church no benefice can exist without being at the same time connected with an ecclesiastical office. There are, however, ecclesiastical offices which are not benefices. This chapter deals exclusively with such offices as are not benefices, except in Article 2, Sec. 3, which includes material on offices which are benefices, and which is applicable likewise to the support received from an ecclesiastical subsidy.

In Canon Law an ecclesiastical office is to be understood in the strict sense, unless it is otherwise obvious from the context of the

---

the principles of Comparative Law are not to be majored, but that the principles of Conflict of Laws are more applicable, because the law to be considered controlling in determining the nature of support of diocesan priests is Canon Law, not American Secular Law, except insofar as the American Law has been adopted as Canon Law by the Church itself.

[4]Zollmann, *American Church Law,* p. 424.

[5]Robert J. White, "American Church Law," *HLR,* XLVII (1933), 378.

[6]An officer of the Army and the Navy does not hold his position by contract, but by a privilege revocable by the sovereign power at will (5 C.J., 316). The position, grade, and rank of officers depend upon the provisions of positive law (5 C.J., 312). A fixed and direct amount of pay is given by statute to officers in the military service (5 C.J., 319). The pay of an officer being fixed by statute, his right to compensation rests on the statute and not on a contract. But his right is legally enforceable and the officer can maintain an action in American secular courts to collect such pay. A priest, on the contrary, cannot maintain any such action in the American secular courts. One may note, in passing, that such non-contractual compensation of military officers has been made expressly subject to taxation by the Public Salary Tax Act of 1939—26 U.S.C. 2530-2531.

[7]Canons 145, 146, 1409, 1413, § 2. Cf. Coronata, *Institutiones* I, 241; Sipos, *Enchiridion,* p. 770; Vermeersch-Creusen, *Epitome,* II, 522; Berutti, *Institutiones,* II, 158-160; Toso, *Commentaria,* II, 111; Regatillo, *Institutiones,* I, 162-163.

canons that the wide sense is intended.[8] Since there is nothing in the Code of Canon Law to indicate that the office to be conferred upon a diocesan priest for his support is an office merely in the wide sense, it follows that an office conferred upon a diocesan priest must bear with it some participation in the ecclesiastical power of orders or of jurisdiction.[9]

An ecclesiastical office can be obtained validly only in consequence of a canonical appointment *(provisio)*, namely the concession of the ecclesiastical office by a competent ecclesiastical authority in accordance with the norms of the Code of Canon Law.[10] The local ordinary has the right of filling all ecclesiastical offices which in his territory can be held by diocesan priests.[11] In filling a vacant office, the ordinary must choose a cleric with the qualities required by the law for that office.[12] When other relative factors are of equal import, then diocesan priests with the academic degree of Licentiate or Doctor in Theology or Canon Law as granted by a Pontifical Faculty or University are entitled to preferential treatment in the appointment to ecclesiastical offices.[13]

The appointment to an ecclesiastical office may be effected by means of an act of free conferral *(libera collatio)*, and this is the ordinary manner in which diocesan priests obtain an ecclesiastical office, by means of the so-called act of institution, upon an ecclesiastical superior's nomination, or a patron's presentation of the

[8]Canon 145, § 2; cf. Coronata, *Institutiones*, I, 239-240; Berutti, *Institutiones*, II, 158-159; Regatillo, *Institutiones*, I, 162-163; Toso, *Commentaria*, II, 111-112.

[9]Cf. note 8, *supra*. The nature of support of a parochial assistant or curate is treated in the following chapter as from a subsidy, since the writer is of the opinion that such a priest does not hold an ecclesiastical office.

[10]Canon 147; cf. Coronata, *Institutiones*, I, 242-245; Berutti, *Institutiones*, II, 187; Regatillo, *Institutiones*, I, 170-171; Toso, *Commentaria*, II, 114-115.

[11]Canon 152; certain restrictions regarding appointment to some benefices are found, e.g., in canon 1435. Cf. Coronata, *Institutiones*, I, 242-245; Berutti, *Institutiones*, II, 204-205, 208-209; Toso, *Commentaria*, II, 121-122.

[12]Canon 153. Cf. Coronata, *Institutiones*, I, 247-252; Sipos, *Enchiridion*, pp. 129-133; Regatillo, *Institutiones*, I, 172; Berutti, *Institutiones*, II, 190, 193, 210; Toso, *Commentaria*, II, 122-123.

[13]Canon 1378; S. C. de Sem. et Stud. Univ., decl. *Cum, vi Constitutionis*, 23 maii 1948—*AAS*, XL (1948) 260; *The Jurist*, VIII (1948), 471-472.

priest who is to obtain the office with the ordinary's approval; by means of an act of confirmation, if the priest is elected to an office; by means of an act of admission to the office, if an ineligible candidate has been postulated for the office; and, finally, by the act of election itself, if the law does not demand any act of confirmation for the result of the election.[14] Any one who on his own authority takes or occupies an ecclesiastical office is *ipso facto* legally incapacitated from holding the office, and is to be punished for his usurpation.[15] The appointment to any ecclesiastical office never can be made by the people or the congregation, or by any cleric who does not possess any jurisdiction.[16]

The determination whether the support received by a diocesan priest from an ecclesiastical office is of the essential nature of "compensation" or of the essential nature of a "gift" involves the following question: Is there at Canon Law, as identified with American Law by canon 1529, a contract under which the priest receives his support?[17] Since compensation results from the existence of a contract between the recipient of money, or of other goods of value, and the payor of such money, if there be such a contract, then at Canon Law in the United States the support received by a priest from an ecclesiastical office would be of the nature of "compensation."

There are only two alternatives at American Law, and for the very same reason also at Canon Law in the United States, in accordance with which money or property normally received by a diocesan priest can be classified according to its nature: compensation and gift. These two concepts are mutually exclusive, so that any bestowal of support must be either the one or the other. It

---

[14]Canon 148. Cf. Coronata, *Institutiones,* I, 245-246; Berutti, *Institutiones,* II, 188-189; Regatillo, *Institutiones,* I, 171-172; Toso; *Commentaria,* II, 115-117.

[15]Canon 2394; Pistocchi, *De Re Beneficiali,* p. 223; Sipos, *Enchiridion,* pp. 141, 741; Blat, *Commentarium,* V, 309-310; Regatillo, *Institutiones,* II, 437; Coronata, *Institutiones,* IV, 670-671.

[16]Cf. canons 109; 147, § 2; 196; 198. Sipos, *Enchiridion,* p. 95; Berutti, *Institutiones,* II, 187, 306, 310, 313, 314; Coronata, *Institutiones,* I, 329-332, IV, 676; Toso, *Commentaria,* II, 163-167; Regatillo, *Institutiones,* I, 202.

[17]*Supra,* Chapter IV, p. 43.

cannot be both.[18] If there is no American Canon Law contract, then the support received by a diocesan priest from his ecclesiastical office is of the nature of a "gift."[19]

Article 2. Does Support of Diocesan Priests from an Ecclesiastical Office Derive through a Contract?

There are at least three cumulative fundamental tests for establishing whether there is at Canon Law in the United States a contract whereby a diocesan priest receives his support from an ecclesiastical office. The non-existence of any one of these precludes the existence of a contract.[20]

(1) The right to discharge the priest from his office.[21]

(2) The right to control the priest as to the details of his priestly work in his office.[22]

(3) The existence of a legally sufficient consideration to bring a contract into being.[23]

Sec. 1. The Right to Discharge a Priest from His Office

The existence of the legal power to discharge is essential to the existence of a contract of employment. The power to discharge a priest from his office is an indicium of the possible existence of some contract of employment whereby he would receive his support.[24] The person possessing such a legal right is called an employer.[25]

It is a doctrine of the Catholic Church, restated in the Code of Canon Law, that no man can be discharged from his priesthood, since the sacrament of Holy Orders whereby a man becomes a priest imprints upon his soul an indelible mark which remains for-

---

18 *Bogardus v. Commissioner of Internal Revenue,* 302 U. S. 34.

19 Cf. *supra,* Chapter IV; cf. *HLR,* XLVII (1933), 1 ff., at p. 11.

20 39 C.J., 35.

21 Cf. 39 C.J., 35-36.

22 Cf. 39 C.J., 33.

23 Cf. *Restatement of Contracts,* § 19, and §§ 75 ff.

24 Cf. 39 C.J., 35-36.

25 20 CFR, Cum. Supp., § 404.104.

ever.[26] An ecclesiastical office, however, can be lost by resignation, deprivation, removal, transfer, or the lapse of the term of appointment.[27] Although an ecclesiastical office can be lost in consequence of the incumbent's resignation of it, in such a case the priest is not discharged from his office but voluntarily relinquishes it. The fact of resignation does not imply the power or authority to discharge a priest from an ecclesiastical office.[28] The only one who under the Canon Law has power to deprive a diocesan priest of an ecclesiastical office is his proper ordinary.[29]

An office may be lost by deprivation. The deprivation of an office may be incurred either automatically in consequence of some ruling in the law itself, or contingently through the act of the legitimate superior. The ordinary cannot deprive an irremovable incumbent of his office except by due process of law. In the case of a removable incumbent of office the deprivation may be decreed by the ordinary for any just reason according to his prudent judgment, even though there be no offence or delict on the part of the cleric. While the ordinary must respect the dictates of natural equity, he is not bound to follow any certain form of procedure except in those cases for which the Code calls for a specific procedure, whether administrative or judicial.[30]

In accordance with the very nature of the loss of an office through an act of transfer the incumbents of ecclesiastical offices are provided a proper support by the ordinary when they thus lose their offices. Transfer indeed involves the loss of one office, but it in-

---

[26]Canon 732, § 1; cf. Sipos, *Enchiridion*, p. 420.

[27]Canon 183, § 1. This is an exhaustive enumeration. Cf. Coronata, *Institutiones*, I, 279; Vermeersch-Creusen, *Epitome*, I, 269; Toso, *Commentaria*, II, 149-151; Sipos, *Enchiridion*, pp. 146-152.

[28]Resignation into the hands of the laity is under penalty forbidden to diocesan priests. Cf. Pistocchi, *De Re Beneficiali*, p. 474; Regatillo, *Institutiones*, II, 437, I, p. 198; Coronata, *Institutiones*, IV, 676; Sipos, *Enchiridion*, p. 148; canon 2400.

[29]The proper ordinary is the bishop of his diocese; The Pope is, of course, under canon 218, § 2, also the proper ordinary of every diocese. Cf. canon 335, § 1; canons 192, 193; Berutti, *Institutiones*, II, 300-303; Regatillo, *Institutiones*, I, 252-253; Toso, *Commentaria*, III, 160-161.

[30]Berutti, *Institutiones*, II, 300-302; Regatillo, *Institutiones*, I, 198; Toso, *Commentaria*, II, 158-160.

herently connotes a subsequent appointment to another office. When an office is lost through the lapse of the time for which the incumbent was appointed, the latter must be given another office, or benefice, or subsidy when his incumbency in the previous office has expired.[31] This follows from the fact that the diocesan priest's title to support does not cease upon the occasion of a transfer or the lapse of the term of appointment.

Removal from an office, whether it be administrative or judicial, penal or non-penal, does not of itself deprive a diocesan priest of the right to support flowing from his title of ordination for the service of the diocese. This is quite a different concept from that of discharge as that concept is used in connection with a contract of employment wherein all right to support ceases on discharge.[32]

The right of a diocesan priest to support continues as long as it is not forfeited through the incurred and inflicted punishment of deposition or of the perpetual privation of the right to wear the ecclesiastical garb. In the former of these two cases, an appeal for support can be based only on the claims of Christian charity; in the latter even such an appeal is no longer acknowledged. It appears, then, that the ordinary must under the dictates of the Code of Canon Law provide in some way for the support of any priest whom he deprives of an ecclesiastical office.[33]

As has been noted above,[33a] in reference to the United States the Sacred Congregation for the Propagation of the Faith in a response on February 4, 1873, to the Bishop of Natchez, a diocese admittedly one of the poorest of the dioceses of this country at the time, required the diocese to provide a fitting support to a priest who had, *through his own fault,* become unworthy of serving a congregation. It was declared that the bishop could not refuse a diocesan priest a fitting support even though his removal from his assignment had

[31]Cf. canons 193 and 981, § 2, as read in connection with canon 979, § 2. Cf. Berutti, *Institutiones,* II, 303; Regatillo, *Institutiones,* I, 198; Toso, *Commentaria,* II, 161.

[32]Cf. 39 C.J., 35, 36; Canons 2299, § 3; 2303; 2304; Regatillo, *Institutiones,* II, 389, 392; Sipos, *Enchiridion,* pp. 945-946; Berutti, *Institutiones,* VI, 229, 233-235.

[33]Cf. *infra,* Chapter VII, Article 6, p. 99.

[33a]Cf. *supra,* p. 66.

been justified, unless after repeated warnings the priest did not amend his life and thus demonstrated his contumacy.[34]

Discharge from office, then, does not deprive a diocesan priest in the United States of his right at Canon Law to a decent support. Since the legal power to discharge a priest from his office and to stop his support is an indicium of the existence of a contract of employment, there does not in the absence of such power exist any contract of employment at Canon Law in the United States, whereby a diocesan priest receives his support from an ecclesiastical office.[35]

Sec. 2. The Right to Control the Priest as to the Details of His Priestly Work in His Office

When the person for whom services are performed has the legal right to control and direct the individual who performs the services not only as to the results to be accomplished by the work but also as to the details and means by which that result is accomplished, there may be the relationship of employer and employee deriving from a contract of employment. That is to say, an employee is subject to the will and control of the employer not only as to what shall be done but also as to how it shall be done. In this connection it is not necessary that the employer actually direct or control the manner in which the services are performed; it is sufficient if he has the right to do so.[36]

All diocesan priests are bound by a special obligation at Canon Law of obeying their ordinary.[37] As often as and whenever in the judgment of their ordinary the needs of the diocese require it, unless there be a legitimate impediment, every diocesan priest must

---

[34]*Collectanea*, n. 1394; *Fontes*, n. 4881.

[35]Cf. 39 C.J., 35, 36. Pope Pius XI, in his encyclical *"Ad Catholici sacerdotii,"* 20 dec. 1935 *(AAS*, XXVIII [1936], 28-29), stated that the Catholic priest is not an "employee."

[36]Cf. 39 C.J., 33; 20 CFR, Cum. Sup., § 404.104.

[37]Canon 127. Cf. Toso, *Commentaria*, II, 84; Berutti, *Institutiones*, II, 119; Regatillo, *Institutiones*, I, 151-152.

take up and faithfully perform any duty entrusted to him by his ordinary.[38]

The authority of the ordinary, however, in directing the details of the priestly work performed in an ecclesiastical office is limited. The ordinary has the power and authority to govern only in accordance with the law.[39] This limits the ordinary's power of direction to the scope of the ecclesiastical laws.[40] The enforcement of the ecclesiastical laws does not of itself give the ordinary any absolute power to direct all the details of the priestly work in an ecclesiastical office.[41]

It has been said that the power of the ordinary to direct his priests in the details of their work is somewhat akin to that of a principal and assistant teacher of a school, one of subordination without agency or service. In *Evangelista v. Ver,* the Supreme Court of the Philippine Islands held that the relationship of officials in a religious denomination to one another is that of ecclesiastical subordination to a common superior, rather than of employer and employee.[42] In the United States it has been held that the relation between a bishop and priest is not that of master and servant, nor that of hirer and hired.[43] Since it is only in the relationship which arises from a contract of employment that the employer has the legal right to direct all the employee's acts, even in detail, the fact that this relationship does not exist at law between a diocesan priest and his bishop is an indicium that there is no contract of employment whereby a priest receives his support.[44]

---

[38]Canon 128. Cf. Berutti, *Institutiones,* II, 121; Toso, *Commentaria,* II, 85; Regatillo, *Institutiones,* I, 152.

[39]Canon 335, § 1; cf. Coronata, *Institutiones,* I, 446-447; Regatillo, *Institutiones,* I, 252-253; Toso, *Commentaria,* III, 160-161.

[40]Canon 336. Cf. Regatillo, *Institutiones,* I, 253-254; Toso, *Commentaria,* III, 161-162.

[41]E.g., the granting, deferring, or refusing of absolution in the sacrament of penance is within the discretion of the priest, subject only to the laws of the Code of Canon Law and the teachings of theology.

[42]8 Philip. 653.

[43]*Baxter v. McDonnell,* 155 N. Y. 83 (1898); *Tuigg v. Sheehan,* 101 Pa. 363 (1882).

[44]Cf. canon 1529; *supra,* Chapter IV.

Sec. 3. The Existence or Absence of a Legally Sufficient Consideration to Bring a Contract into Being

A legally sufficient consideration is essential to the existence at Canon Law in the United States of any and every contract.[45] The fact that a sum is received by a priest for his support does not necessarily constitute a legally sufficient consideration. To be legally sufficient, a consideration must imply an exchange or price requested and received by the priest in exchange for the religious services which he performs in the course of his office.[46] The Supreme Court of the United States in a gift tax case, under a statute, has declared that a legally sufficient consideration is that which can be valued in "money or money's worth."[47]

Considering this point in relation to the diocesan priesthood, the Supreme Court of the State of Pennsylvania declared in *Tuigg v. Sheehan:*

> The moving consideration in such contracts is the pecuniary advantage flowing from the relation. When a priest dedicates his life to the Church and takes upon himself the vows of obedience to its laws, he is presumed to be actuated by a higher principle than the hope of gain.[48]

The words of Pope Pius XI in his encyclical letter on the Catholic Priesthood indicate the official position of the Church regarding diocesan priests:

> The Catholic priest ought to be distinguished by his detachment. Surrounded by the corruptions of a world in which everything can be bought and sold, he must pass through them

---

[45]Cf. canon 1529; *supra*, Chapter IV; cf. Vromant, *De Bonis Ecclesiae*, p. 294; Wernz-Vidal, *Ius Canonicum*, IV, II, 332; Blat; *Commentarium*, IV, 546; Cocchi, *Commentarium*, VI, 410-411; all of these commentators state that the most authoritative legal experts of the place are to be consulted. Williston *(Contracts*, I, § 99) offers the best commentary on the American Canon Law of Contracts.

[46]*Restatement of Contracts*, §§ 80 ff.

[47]*Merrill v. Fahs*, 324 U. S. 308 (1945); *Commissioner v. Wemyss*, 324 U. S. 303 (1945). The absence of a consideration is not necessarily the same as the lack of a *quid pro quo*. *Weagant v. Bowers*, 57 F. 2d 679. Cf. 51 C.J., 124 re: Remunerative Gifts, *supra*, p. 49.

[48]101 Pa. 363 (1882).

utterly free of selfishness. He must holily spurn all vile greed of earthly gains, since he is in search of souls, not of money; of the glory of God, not his own. He is no mercenary working for a temporal recompense, nor yet an employee who, whilst attending conscientiously to duties of his office, at the same time is looking to his career and personal promotion.[49]

The Bishop of Bardstown (Louisville) asked the Sacred Congregation for the Propagation of the Faith in 1816 what was the best method of providing for the support of diocesan priests in the United States. The Sacred Congregation replied that the priests were to receive their support from the "voluntary offerings of the faithful."[50] This same Sacred Congregation was also asked what was the nature of the obligation of the laity to supply support for diocesan priests. In the reply given, no mention of any enforceable obligation at law, whether Canon or Secular, was made. Instead, it was simply stated that the faithful are obliged "in conscience" to provide a sufficient support for the priests of the Church.[51] Moreover, priests were expressly forbidden to attempt to enforce the payment of any sums for their support by refusing to baptize the children of Catholic families until the parents had made payment for the support of the priests.[52]

The moral obligation "in conscience" to provide support for diocesan priests is not a legally sufficient consideration.[53] Since it is a *sine qua non* requisite of Canon Law in the United States that for the formation of a contract there be a legally sufficient consideration given for the promise or promises therein,[54] and since there is no legally sufficient consideration whereby a priest receives his support, it follows that there is in the United States no contract under which he receives support.

---

[49] *AAS,* XXVIII (1936), 28-29 (Vatican Press Translation).

[50] Ad 2 *Collectanea,* n. 713; *Fontes,* n. 4705.

[51] Ad 3 *Collectanea,* n. 713; *Fontes,* n. 4705.

[52] Ad 4 *Collectanea,* n. 713; *Fontes,* n. 4705.

[53] Williston, *Contracts,* I, § 147.

[54] Canon 1529; Williston, *Contracts,* I, § 111; *supra,* Chapter IV.

Article 3. No Contract by Which a Priest Receives His Support Exists Between a Priest and His Bishop

The existence of a Canon Law-American Law contract between a priest and his bishop under which a priest obtains a legally enforceable right to support has been asserted. The matter has been brought to the American secular courts of last resort on three occasions, but on these three occasions the American courts have given judgments that there is no such contract between a priest and bishop.[55] Under canon 1529 these decisions of the American courts are recognized, adopted, and given effect as Canon Law in the United States, with the same extent and scope they have under American Secular Law.

The question of fact to be decided in the case of *Alphonse Rose v. John Vertin* was: Did there exist between the bishop and the priest a contract of employment at American Law imposing upon the bishop personally an enforceable obligation to pay the priest a salary for the services rendered by him to his parish? The Supreme Court of the State of Michigan declared that there was no contract at American law between the bishop and the priest. The Court, through Judge Graves, stated in part:

> The relation between Bishop Mrack and the priest was never that of hirer and hired in any sense implying an obligation of the bishop to pay the priest. The bishop was the priest's superior, and according to the established order of things in the economy of the church government, regulating the degree of subordination and methods of administration, it was the province of the bishop to designate the place for the priest to exercise his functions, and prescribe under certain limitations the rules and precepts for his guidance and control. . . . In the course of administration the bishop assigned to the priest a theatre of duty and gave him certain rules and instructions, and it was manifestly understood on both sides that the bishop was not to be responsible in law for the salary . . .

In *Tuigg v. Sheehan*, the Rev. Patrick M. Sheehan brought suit on the grounds of an implied contract against the Bishop of Pitts-

[55] *Alphonse Rose v. John Vertin*, 46 Mich. 457 (1881); *Tuigg v. Sheehan*, 101 Pa. 363 (1882); *Baxter v. McDonnell*, 155 N. Y. 83 (1898).

burgh. The question before the Court was: Does a contract, either express or implied, whether implied in law or in fact, exist between a priest and his bishop? The Supreme Court of the State of Pennsylvania stated that there was no such contract between the parties. The Court said in part:

> *It would be doing a wrong to the Catholic Church and degrade its priesthood from their high position were we to hold that the relation between the bishop and his priest was that of hirer and hired, or employer and employee.*[56] The moving consideration in such contracts is the pecuniary advantage flowing from the relation. When a priest dedicates his life to the Church . . . he is presumed to be actuated by a higher principle than the hope of gain.[57]

In *Baxter v. McDonnell,* Father Baxter sued his bishop on the grounds that there was between the bishop and himself as priest an implied contract (i.e., a quasi-contract) obliging the bishop to support him. The New York Court of Appeals decided in the negative. It stated that no contract, either express or implied, exists in the case of a priest in relation to his bishop.[58]

Zollman, the only American author who to any degree deals extensively with this subject, states that attempts by priests to assert that a contract existed with their bishop have met with no favor in the secular courts.[59] Since there is no contract at American Law, it follows that there cannot be any contract at Canon Law in the United States whereby a priest receives his support, for under canon 1529 the American Law on contracts and payments is adopted by the Code of Canon Law as the law of the Catholic Church in the United States.[60] The duty of the Church to support its priests bears some analogy to the obligation which is recognized by several religious denominations with reference to the support of their own poor. Yet it has never been supposed that

[56]Emphasis inserted. Cf. Pius XI, litt. encycl. *Ad Catholici sacerdotii,* 20 dec. 1935—*AAS,* XXVIII (1936), 28-29, in which Pope Pius XI stated that the Catholic priest is no "employee."

[57]101 Pa. 363 (1882).

[58]155 N. Y. 83 (1898).

[59]*American Church Law,* p. 451.

[60]Cf. *supra,* Chapter IV.

this duty involved a contractual relation which would sustain an action at law for its non-performance.[61]

Article 4. Is Support from an Ecclesiastical Office of the Nature of a "Gift"?

The support received by a diocesan priest in the United States from an ecclesiastical office comes from the voluntary contributions of the faithful.[62] There is no legal liability on the part of the Catholic faithful to contribute any specific amount towards the support of the diocesan priests, and whatever obligation the laity have is only a generic one binding *simply in conscience.*[63] When assigned by his bishop to an ecclesiastical office, the priest does not enter into any contract of employment, or into any other type of contract, whether express or implied, with the laity, who are precluded from any ecclesiastical jurisdiction by canon 118, and who do not have the superior choice, control, and direction of the priest in the performance of his duties as a priest,[64] and hence cannot discharge him or remove him from office.

When there is no contractual relation between the parties, or any legal obligation of the payor to the recipient, then payments constitute gifts.[65] Since under the American Canon Law there are only the two alternatives in accordance with which money or property received by a diocesan priest for his support can be classified according to its nature, i.e., as compensation or as a gift, and since the support received from an ecclesiastical office is not a contractual compensation, it is of necessity of the nature of a "gift" at both Canon Law and American Civil Law.[66]

---

[61] Zollmann, *American Church Law,* 487. *Qui dat pauperibus, Deo dat.* 51 C.J., 124.

[62] S. C. de Prop. Fide, 13 maii 1816, ad 2—*Collectanea,* n. 713; *Fontes,* n. 4705.

[63] *Ibid.,* ad 3—*loc. cit.*

[64] The laity have, under canon 682, simply *ad normam ecclesiasticae disciplinae,* the right to receive from the priest spiritual aids to salvation.

[65] *Weagant v. Bowers,* 57 F. 2d 679 (1932); Mertens, *Taxation,* I, § 8.08.

[66] *Supra,* Chapter IV.

CHAPTER VII

THE NATURE OF SUPPORT OF DIOCESAN PRIESTS FROM A SUBSIDY

ARTICLE 1. PRELIMINARY NOTIONS

The ordinary must confer upon each priest whom he promotes on the title of service of the diocese a benefice, or an office, or *a subsidy* sufficient for his adequate support.[1] The source of this subsidy in the United States is the voluntary offerings of the faithful—offerings made to a parish or a diocesan benefice—a portion of which is assigned by the ordinary to the priest for his adequate support.[2] This subsidy is to be granted to those diocesan priests who do not hold an ecclesiastical benefice or office which provides them with an adequate support.

ARTICLE 2. DIOCESAN PRIESTS ASSIGNED TO ECCLESIASTICAL DUTIES NOT PROVIDING ADEQUATE SUPPORT FROM A BENEFICE OR AN OFFICE

SEC. 1. PRELIMINARY NOTIONS

At times diocesan priests are assigned by their ordinaries to duties which do not provide an adequate support from an ecclesiastical benefice or an ecclesiastical office.[3] In such cases the sup-

[1]Canon 981, § 2 (italics inserted; translation by the writer); Vermeersch-Creusen, *Epitome,* II, 143; Sipos, *Enchiridion,* p. 447.

[2]Cf. Allen, *Existentia Beneficiorum,* pp. 109-110; Hannan, "The Cleric's Last Will," *The Jurist,* VIII (1948), 59-60. This is a different situation from that in certain European countries in which the civil government by act of its legislature has enacted statutes under which the priests receive a subsidy from the public treasury—a subsidy which may be legally enforceable by action in the secular courts of these countries. Cf. Vromant, *De Bonis Ecclesiae,* pp. 213-214.

[3]Examples of such assignments, not listed all-inclusive here, are the assignment of priests to the staff of a diocesan curia or to parishes as

port of these priests comes by way of an ecclesiastical subsidy.[4] The diocesan priest has a right at Canon Law to receive this subsidy.[5]

SEC. 2. IS SUPPORT FROM SAID SUBSIDY OF THE NATURE OF "COMPENSATION"?

Support received by diocesan priests in the United States as such a subsidy must, under American Canon Law, come to the priest either under a contract or not under a contract. A contract at American Canon Law is a promise, or a set of promises, for the breach of which the law gives a remedy, or the performance of which the law in some way recognizes as a duty.[6] An additional *sine qua non* factor for the existence of a contract is that there must be a legally sufficient consideration.[7]

---

assistant pastors. Cf. Manning, *The Free Conferral of Offices*, The Catholic University of America Canon Law Studies, n. 219 (Washington, D. C.; The Catholic University of America Press, 1945), p. 93. No treatment of the support of diocesan priests from contractual positions assumed by them as instructors or professors in certain Catholic universities and colleges is herein included. It is the opinion of the writer that many such diocesan priests on the faculties of universities and colleges may well receive their support in exactly the same manner as any lay teacher receives his support from the same position—by a contract at American Law, both Canon and Secular, and enforceable in the courts of both systems of law. This is quite a different legal status from that of diocesan priests receiving support from an ecclesiastical subsidy in which no contractual relation exists.

[4]In the United States this ecclesiastical subsidy is generally called, in accordance with the usage of the word in the III Plenary Council of Baltimore, decree no. 273, a priest's "salary" as the equivalent of the term "*congrua*"—the technical ecclesiastical term for such support assigned to the priest by his ordinary; cf. *supra*, p. 18. It must constantly be borne in mind that "salary" is not a univocal word with but one meaning in law. At post-Code Canon Law in the United States, identified with the American Secular law by canon 1529, it can and does mean either: 1) compensation coming from a contract (cf. 54 C.J., 1124) or 2) under the Baltimore legislation still in force, the "*congrua*" or "*portio congrua*"—a non-contractual transfer to the priest for his support, which transfer derives from funds voluntarily contributed by the laity to the Church for that purpose. Cf. canon 1496. Cf. *supra*, pp. 17, 27.

[5]Canon 981, § 2; Vermeersch-Creusen, *Epitome*, II, 143.

[6]*Restatement of Contracts*, § 1.

[7]Williston, *Contracts*, I, § 99.

No promise or set of promises is made by the priest to anyone in the acceptance of his assignment by his ordinary to such duties in the service of his diocese as do not provide him with adequate support from an ecclesiastical benefice or office.[8] Nor are promises made by the ordinary to the priest. The ordinary, in the course of good administration of his diocese, simply assigns the priest to a specific duty, which duty the priest accepts. The assignment is made by virtue of the authority vested in the ordinary as stated in canons 335 and 336. It is accepted by the priest in obedience to what is demanded of him according to the statements contained in canons 127 and 128. Having accepted the assignment, the priest faithfully fulfills, in obedience to the law as stated in canon 128, the charge committed to him. The intention of both the ordinary and the priest is to comply with the provisions of the Code of Canon Law. Neither has any intention to enter into a relationship to be governed by the laws of the State, or by any laws save those of the Church. Certainly neither the priest nor the ordinary has any intention, recognized by the Code of Canon Law, to enter into a situation which entails secular legal consequences which may be contrary to the provisions of the Code of Canon Law, yet such would be the consequences which flow from a valid contract at American Law whereby the priest would be enabled to sue his ordinary in the secular courts to enforce payment of support, and the ordinary would be enabled to sue the priest to enforce *by secular law* the satisfactory fulfillment of the religious duties assigned to him. Such a yielding of jurisdiction by the Church with reference to the support of diocesan priests is beyond the competence of either bishops or priests in view of canon 1553 § 1.[9] When no promises are made, the intention of the parties remains the controlling factor regarding the nature of any payment.[10]

To produce a contract, moreover, a legally sufficient consideration is requisite. Such a consideration implies an exchange or a price requested and received by a promisor for a promise, a legal

[8]Two parties are necessary for constituting the existence of a contractual promise. Hence a priest cannot by a promise to himself create a contract.

[9]Cf. Roberti, *Respectus Sociales,* p. 50.

[10]Mertens, *Taxation,* I § 8.08.

detriment incurred by the promisee at the request of the promisor as the price for the promise, or the legal benefit received by the promisor.[11] No legal detriment is incurred in this transaction by either the priest or the ordinary. The services of the priest, spiritual in their nature, are rendered in his search for souls, not of money; of the glory of God, not his own. The priest in receiving a subsidy is no mercenary working for temporal recompense.[12] The motive of both the ordinary and the priest to achieve the salvation of souls is no legal detriment and hence not legally sufficient consideration.[13] Nor is the moral obligation in conscience upon both ordinary and priest so to act legally sufficient consideration.[14] In the absence of any promise and of any legally sufficient consideration, no contract at American Canon Law can exist whereby a diocesan priest receives his support from such ecclesiastical subsidy.[15] Since such subsidy is not contractual in its character it, by consequence, cannot be of the nature, at law in the United States, "compensation." [16]

SEC. 3. IS SUPPORT FROM SAID SUBSIDY OF THE NATURE OF A "GIFT"?

When there is no contractual relation between the parties, then payments constitute gifts.[17] There is no contractual relation at American Canon Law whereby a diocesan priest receives his support from a subsidy.[18] There is no legal obligation at American Secular Law whereby a priest receives such a subsidy.[19] There is, of course, a fundamental right under the Natural Law, the Divine Positive Law, and Canon Law, though non-contractual in its character, whereby a diocesan priest receives such a subsidy.[20]

---

[11]Williston, *Contracts,* I § 102.

[12]Cf. Pius XI, litt. encycl. *"Ad Catholici sacerdotii,"* 20 dec. 1935—*AAS,* XXVIII (1936), 5, at pp. 28-29.

[13]Cf. *supra.* p. 47; cf. Williston, *Contracts,* I, § 147.

[14]Cf. Williston, *Contracts,* I, § 147.

[15]Cf. Zollmann, *American Church Law,* 453.

[16]Cf. *supra,* Chapter IV.

[17]*Weagant v. Bowers,* 57 F. 2d 679 (1932); Mertens, *Taxation,* I, § 8.08.

[18]*Supra,* sec. 2.

[19]*Tuigg v. Sheehan,* 101 Pa. 363.

[20]Canon 981, § 2; Vermeersch-Creusen, *Epitome,* II, 143; cf. *supra,* Chapter III, Art. 2.

Since there does not exist at American Canon Law any contract whereby a diocesan priest receives his support from a subsidy, it follows that whatever money or bank checks or other goods of value he receives as an ecclesiastical subsidy, under whatever name it may be called, is of the nature of a "gift."

Article 3. Diocesan Priests Assigned to Advanced Studies

Sec. 1. Preliminary Notions

Under the Code of Canon Law it is desirable that ordinaries assign diocesan priests, outstanding for their piety and ability, to Universities or Faculties approved by the Holy See, for postgraduate studies in scripture, philosophy, theology, or canon law, with a view to gaining an ecclesiastical academic degree.[21] Ordinaries in the United States, realizing the mind of the Church in this matter, do in fact so assign diocesan priests for advanced studies in these and other fields.

These priests were ordained on the title of service to the diocese;[22] they are priests upon whom the ordinary is obliged by the Code of Canon Law to confer a benefice, an office, or a subsidy sufficient for their adequate support.[23] Since in the United States a priest who has been assigned for advanced studies will generally attend a University or a Faculty outside his own diocese, it will normally be impossible for his ordinary to confer upon such a priest any residential benefice or ecclesiastical office. Accordingly, diocesan priests assigned for advanced studies are to be supported by means of a subsidy which must be conferred upon them by their ordinary.[24]

Prior to the Code of Canon Law that portion of ecclesiastical revenues which was assigned by the ordinary to a cleric as a subsidy while he was engaged in advanced studies was called a "*praestimonium*" or at times the "*portio praestimonialis.*" [25] This subsidy,

---

[21]Canon 1380. Cf. Vermeersch-Creusen, *Epitome,* II, 412.

[22]Cf. Wernz-Vidal, *Ius Canonicum,* IV, I, p. 298, n. 310.

[23]Canon 981, § 2; Vermeersch-Creusen, *Epitome,* II, 143.

[24]Canon 981, § 2: "Ordinarius . . . *debet* . . . [subsidium] . . . conferre."

[25]F. Santi, *Praelectiones Juris Canonici* (2 vols., Ratisbon, New York and Cincinnati: Pustet, 1886), Lib. III, tit. 5, n. 34; cf. Coronata, *Institutiones,* II, 359.

after the Code, is normally not an ecclesiastical pension.[26] D'Angelo (1885-1930) asserted that this subsidy can be granted by an ordinary as an ecclesiastical pension derivable from the income of the parish in which the priest was a *vicarius cooperator* before the ordinary assigned him to advanced studies, but he counseled that the ordinary obtain the permission of the Holy See before he grants the subsidy from such a source in the form of an ecclesiastical pension.[27] The subsidy generally will be a direct grant-in-aid for the support of the diocesan priest, and generally also will be derived from the funds of the diocesan curia.

The amount of the subsidy which a diocesan priest assigned to advanced studies *must* be granted by his ordinary is that amount which will *de facto* be truly sufficient for that priest's adequate support.[28] The determination of the amount necessary for this adequate support is a question of fact, and the amount will, of necessity, vary from priest to priest, year to year, and place to place. The minimum as set by the Code of Canon Law is that amount which is truly necessary for the priest's adequate support. No more than is truly necessary needs to be granted by the ordinary for his compliance with what the Code of Canon Law demands as a minimum, since the subsidy is *ad sustentandum sacerdotem, non ad ditandum eum.* The granting of a subsidy slightly in excess of the bare minimum required by the Code of Canon Law will ensure a more efficient utilization of the opportunities for advanced studies, since the diocesan priest will thus be freed from many worries and cares which otherwise might result for him.

While the amount of the subsidy is a question of fact, the *nature* of the subsidy conferred upon diocesan priests assigned to advanced studies is, however, a question of law, and will remain

---

[26]S. Gass, *Ecclesiastical Pensions,* The Catholic University of America Canon Law Studies, no. 157 (Washington, D. C.: The Catholic University of America Press, 1942), p. 124.

[27]S. D'Angelo, *Le Tasse e le Pensioni nel Codice di diritto Canonico* (2. ed., cor. ed ampl., Torino: L.I.C.E., 1927) § 122, n. 2 (hereafter cited *Tasse e Pensioni).*

[28]Canon 981, § 2; Vermeersch-Creusen, *Epitome,* II, 143; Sipos, *Enchiridion,* p. 447.

constant in the United States so long as the provisions of canon 1529 are not changed.[29]

SEC. 2. IS SUPPORT OF DIOCESAN PRIESTS ASSIGNED TO ADVANCED STUDIES OF THE NATURE OF "COMPENSATION"?

For the support of diocesan priests assigned to advanced studies to be of the nature of compensation it is required that said support be received by reason of a contract.[30] For the existence of a contract at American Canon Law there is required a promise, or a set of promises, for the breach of which the law gives a remedy, or for the performance of which the law in some way recognizes or establishes a duty.[31] In addition, a legally sufficient consideration is a *sine qua non* factor for the existence of any contract.[32]

When a diocesan priest is assigned to advanced studies there is, in such an assignment, no promise made to the priest by the ordinary. The assignment is made in the same manner as if the priest were to be appointed to any position in the diocese.[33] The ordinary, under the authority vindicated for him in the Code of Canon Law, and for the efficient administration of the diocese, simply orders the priest to go to a specified University or Faculty and there study a specified subject.[34] The priest makes no promise to the ordinary with reference to the future support. He simply obeys the orders given him.[35]

There is no intent in the mind of either the ordinary or the diocesan priest to enter into a contract valid at Canon and Ameri-

[29]A payment of money is a payment of money in Rome and in Washington, yet canonically the legal understanding and treatment of that payment in the two places may well be very different because of canon 1529. Cf. *supra,* Chapter III, Art. 1.

[30]*Supra,* Chapter IV, Art. 2.

[31]*Restatement of Contracts,* § 1.

[32]Williston, *Contracts,* I, § 99.

[33]Cf. canon 128; Blat, *Commentarium,* II, 82.

[34]Cf. canon 335; Blat, *Commentarium,* II, 350-351. The mere fact that the order may be phrased softly as a request to the priest to go to a University does not change its nature from that of an order by an ecclesiastical superior to his subordinate.

[35]Cf. canon 127; Blat, *Commentarium,* II, 81.

can Law, with all the legal consequences which flow therefrom, such as would leave room for the ordinary or the diocese to be sued on a contract by the priest for support in the secular or ecclesiastical courts, or for the priest to be sued on a contract by the bishop in the secular or ecclesiastical courts with the view of coercing him to study more zealously and to obtain higher academic grades in his studies. The intention of both is to comply with the laws of the Church. In the case of the ordinary the intention is to comply with the ruling of canon 1380, while in the case of the priest the intention is to comply with the rulings of canons 127 and 128. These canons make no provisions whatsoever for any promises for the breach of which the law gives a remedy, or for the performance of which the law in some way recognizes or establishes a duty arising from a contract enforceable by judicial action.

It is a *sine qua non* requisite of American Canon Law for the existence of a contract that a legally sufficient consideration be given for the promise or promises therein. The fundamental idea is that the consideration implies an exchange or price requested and received by the promisor for the promise. It implies in substance a legal detriment incurred by the promisee at the request of the promisor as the price for the promise, or the legal benefit received by the promisor. Benefit and detriment have a technical meaning. Detriment as used in a testing of the sufficiency of a consideration denotes a legal detriment as distinguished from a detriment in fact. It means: (a) giving up something which immediately prior thereto the promisee was privileged to keep, or (b) doing a thing or refraining from something which the promisee then was privileged not to do or not to refrain from doing. And benefit correspondingly means the receiving as the exchange for his promise of some performance or forbearance which the promisor was not previously entitled to receive.[36]

Since no promises are made regarding the support of a diocesan priest assigned to advanced studies, there cannot be any legally sufficient consideration given or received in connection therewith. Moreover, no legal detriment is incurred by either the priest or

[36]Cf. *supra,* Chapter IV, Art. 2.; Williston, *Contracts,* I, § 102.

the ordinary.[37] Instead, both are simply complying with the law of the Code. Compliance with the law of the Code does not constitute a legal detriment or benefit. Hence there cannot be any legally sufficient consideration in the case. Accordingly at American Canon Law there cannot exist any contract whereby a diocesan priest assigned to advanced studies receives a subsidy for his support.[38] Since there is no contract whereby a diocesan priest assigned to advanced studies receives a subsidy for his support, it follows that such a subsidy is not of the nature of compensation.[39]

SEC. 3. IS THE SUPPORT OF PRIESTS ASSIGNED TO ADVANCED STUDIES OF THE NATURE OF A "GIFT"?

At Canon Law there rests upon the ordinary the obligation (not of a contractual nature as in the case of a necessitated compensation) to provide the priest with a subsidy truly sufficient for his support.[40] Ordinaries do in fact confer upon such a priest money, bank checks, or other goods of value, as a subsidy for his support.

When there is a transfer of money or bank checks or other goods of value made voluntarily without any contractual obligation, such a transfer is at American Canon Law of the nature of a gift.[41] Since the transfer of a subsidy sufficient for the support of diocesan priests assigned to advanced studies is not accompanied with any contractual obligation, it is, at American Canon Law, of the nature of a gift.[42]

---

[37] Cf. Williston, *Contracts,* I, § 102A.

[38] Cf. Zollmann, *American Church Law,* p. 453.

[39] Cf. *supra,* Chapter IV, Art. 2.

[40] Cf. canon 981, § 2; Vermeersch-Creusen, *Epitome,* II, 143.

[41] *Supra,* Chapter IV, Art. 3; 28 C.J., 620; 26 U.S.C. § 1002.

[42] European Canon Law, following the law of the territory, will treat the transaction differently in consequence of the ruling of canon 1529, and some European commentators speak of such subsidy as a form of remuneration. Remuneration of a non-contractual nature is one of the subclassifications of the genus "gift." Subclassifications are utilized under the European Civil Law, but not at American Law, Common or statutory, except in the State of Louisiana, where a remunerative gift is provided for in Article 1525 of the Compiled Codes of that State. Cf. Chapter IV, Article 3, *supra,* p. 53.

Article 4. The Nature of Support of Priests Incapacitated by Illness

sec. 1. preliminary notions

For diocesan priests incapacitated by illness who are thereby unable to hold a benefice or an office, the Code of Canon Law provides that a subsidy must be conferred upon them by their ordinary. The Code does not determine the method by which such a subsidy shall be conferred.[43] Legislation of the III Plenary Council of Baltimore (1884), which is still in force throughout the United States,[44] ordered on the part of the bishops after taking counsel with the diocesan clergy the adoption of suitable means whereby there would be provided subsidies sufficient for the decent support of the sick priests.[45]

The Council ordered that a fund for this purpose be established from an assessment imposed upon each parish. If, however, in the judgment of the bishop it was deemed imprudent to burden the congregation with this additional request for money, the fund was to be raised by means of an annual assessment, called a tax, to be imposed upon the priests individually. In consequence of this assessment each priest would pay into the fund a fixed percentage of the total so-called salary received by him during the year. This provision of the Plenary Council did not establish an ecclesiastical pension in the juridic sense.[46]

sec. 2. are incapacitated priests supported by contractual compensation?

Transfer to an incapacitated priest of money for his support must, at Canon Law in the United States, be either of the nature

---

[43]Canon 981, § 2.

[44]Barrett, *Comparative Study,* p. 101.

[45]III Plenary Council of Baltimore, decrees nn. 71, 72. "Etiam pro iis sacerdotibus errantibus qui spem emendationis praestant et scandalum allatum reparare volunt."

[46]Cf. Augustine, *The Canonical and Civil Status of Catholic Parishes in the United States* (St. Louis: Herder Book Co., 1926) pp. 49-52; Gass, *Ecclesiastical Pensions,* p. 110. Whether the levying of such a tax is contrary to the Code is outside the scope of this study.

of compensation or of the nature of a gift. To be of the nature of compensation there is required a contract.[47] For the existence of a contract at American Canon Law, in addition to a promise or set of promises, there is required a legally sufficient consideration.[48] A moral obligation or a moral consideration is not a legally sufficient consideration to create a contract at Canon Law in the United States.[49]

The III Plenary Council of Baltimore, in legislating on the subsidy to be granted to incapacitated priests, indicated that the obligation is a moral one based upon the "love and veneration" in which the priests are to be held.[50] The subsidy is to be granted to the priests in order that their affliction may not be aggravated by their poverty, and that they may not be oppressed by temporal solicitudes, but also that they may be cheered in their old age and alleviated in their illness in view of all freedom from worry over money to pay their bills. No contractual intent on the part of the council is indicated in the legislation. No provision for any promises of any type whatsoever is made. Instead, the granting of the subsidy is based upon the Scriptural statement of St. Paul to Timothy that the clergy are to be held worthy of honor.[51]

Since the obligation to grant the subsidy for the support of incapacitated priests is based upon the love and veneration in which priests are to be held, and since "love and veneration" are not reducible to a money value, there is no sufficient consideration to bring a Canon Law contract into existence in the support of said priests. Non-contractual sums are not of the nature of compensation, and accordingly the support received by incapacitated priests is likewise not of the nature of compensation.[52]

---

[47]Cf. *supra,* Chapter IV, Art. 3.

[48]*Restatement of Contracts,* § 1; Williston, *Contracts,* I, § 99.

[49]Williston, *Contracts,* § 147; cf. *supra,* Chapter IV.

[50]III Plenary Council of Baltimore, Decree n. 70.

[51]I Tim., VI, 8.

[52]Cf. *supra,* Chapter IV. Cf. Williston, *Contracts,* I, § 147; 26 U.S.C. § 1002; 26 CFR, Cum. Supp. § 86.8.

SEC. 3. ARE INCAPACITATED PRIESTS SUPPORTED BY GIFTS?

When there is no contractual relation between the parties, the payments constitute gifts.[53] Since there is no contractual relation whereby incapacitated diocesan priests receive support, the money received by them is of the nature of a gift.[54]

ARTICLE 5. THE NATURE OF SUPPORT OF DIOCESAN PRIESTS FROM AN ECCLESIASTICAL PENSION

SEC. 1. PRELIMINARY NOTIONS

An ecclesiastical pension connotes the right to receive each year a part of the fruits deriving from a benefice not one's own (or from other ecclesiastical revenue). There must be present a just cause when an ecclesiastical superior establishes such a pension in behalf of a priest.[55] It is not connected with any office, but rather given for support.[56]

Spiritual pensions are conferred upon clerics while rendering services of a spiritual nature.[57] A pension is a *portio congrua* which

---

[53]*Weagant v. Bowers,* 57 F2d 679 (1932); Mertens, *Taxation,* I, § 8.08.

[54]Cf. *supra,* Chapter IV. Some European writers, following their civil law, speak of said subsidy as a form of remuneration. The distinction in Canon Law in the United States between contractual remuneration (technically of the nature of compensation) and a non-contractual remuneration, a gift *causa remunerationis,* (technically of the nature of a gift) must be borne in mind when one reads their statements. Cf. 54 C.J., 337; cf. *supra,* p. 49.

[55]"Ius percipiendi singulis annis partem fructuum ex alieno beneficio (vel aliis proventibus ecclesiasticis) auctoritate competentis Superioris ecclesiastici cuipiam clerico iusta de causa constitutum."—Cf. F. Wernz, *Ius Decretalium* (6 vols., Romae et Prati, 1898-1905), II, p. 432, n. III. Cf. Sipos, *Enchiridion,* p. 734; Pistocchi, *De Re Beneficiali,* pp. 35-36.

[56]Gass (*Ecclesiastical Pensions,* p. 6) asserts that the term honorarium, emolument, compensation, or a similar one might be more correctly applied. It is respectfully submitted that Gass was not applying canon 1529 in making this statement, for each of these terms has a highly technical meaning at American Canon Law identified with American Secular Law with reference to contracts and payments. Gass, rather than using the words in a technical legal sense, was using them, it is suggested, in a sense accommodated to the common and casual form of conversation.

[57]The State has no jurisdiction over spiritual matters, for these are reserved exclusively to the Church. Cf. canon 1553.

derives from a benefice, or from some other ecclesiastical revenues, and is assigned by the ordinary to a priest for his support. An ecclesiastical pension conferred upon diocesan priests can be made a subsidiary title of ordination;[58] it can also be conferred in remuneration for a present spiritual ministry to which no benefice or office is joined, or by way of temporary maintenance, e.g., while a priest is assigned to advanced studies, or in behalf of an aged or incapacitated cleric.[59]

A clerical pension is given for support—the provision of an adequate maintenance. When the ordinary grants a pension it is required that there be a just cause for his so doing.[60] This cause is to be determined according to the prudent judgment of the ordinary.[61] A pension is a personal right, the purpose of which is to maintain the cleric in a condition becoming the dignity of the clerical state.[62] The holder of an ecclesiastical pension does not have absolute dominion thereof, for the *ius disponendi* is limited in that the pension cannot be alienated or assigned to others.[63]

SEC. 2. IS THE SUPPORT OF DIOCESAN PRIESTS FROM AN ECCLESIASTICAL PENSION OF THE NATURE OF "COMPENSATION"?

Compensation, as regards the support of diocesan priests, must arise at Canon Law in the United States from the existence of a contract.[64] In addition to a promise or promises exchanged between two parties there is necessary for the existence of a contract a legally sufficient consideration.[65] In some cases of statutory gifts,

---

[58]Cf. canon 979, § 4; Cappello, *Tractatus Canonico-moralis de Sacramentis* (3 vols. in 6, Vol. II, Pars. III, *De Sacra Ordinatione,* Taurinorum Augustae: Marietti, 1935), Vol. II, Pars. III, n. 426 (hereafter cited as *De Sacramentis)*; Pistocchi, *De Re Beneficiali,* p. 156.

[59]Gass, *Ecclesiastical Pensions,* p. 4.

[60]Pistocchi, *De Re Beneficiali,* p. 142; cf. canon 1429.

[61]Blat, *Commentarium,* IV, 409.

[62]Pistocchi, *De Re Beneficiali,* p. 142.

[63]Pistocchi, *De Re Beneficiali,* p. 155. It may be noted that Pistocchi *(ibid.,* p. 140) cites Italian and Austrian civil law *as the Canon Law* on pensions in those countries. However, in the United States the government has enacted no such laws which can be considered a part of Canon Law.

[64]*Supra,* Chapter IV.

[65]Williston, *Contracts,* I, § 99; *Restatement of Contracts,* § 1.

a consideration not reducible to a money value is deemed not legally sufficient consideration for the formation of a valid contract.[66]

The ecclesiastical pension is conferred in compliance with the prescriptions of Canon Law, either in recognition of some spiritual service rendered in the past, or as a subsistence to one actually engaged in the present performance of spiritual activities.[67] Herein there is no legally sufficient consideration reducible to a money value.[68] Setting a money value on spiritual services[69] involves the determination of a temporal price for an intrinsically spiritual thing, or for any temporal thing annexed to the spiritual in such a manner that the spiritual thing be even the partial object of the contract. This is simony in the Divine Law.[70]

It is quite different from the legitimate practice in the Church of allowing a temporal amount to be *given*, not *for*, but *on the occasion of*, a spiritual ministry or service.[71] No money value can be placed upon spiritual services, because they cannot, under the Divine Law, be reducible to a temporal money value. Spiritual services, there-

---

[66]26 U.S.C. § 1002; 26 CFR, Cum. Supp., § 86.8.

[67]Cf. Gass, *Ecclesiastical Pensions*, pp. 3-4; Pistocchi, *De Re Beneficiali*, p. 137. The same type of treatment that was used for ascertaining the nature of the support of a diocesan priest which derives from a benefice or an office is here applicable. To avoid multiple repetition, however, the present treatment is utilized. It is equally applicable to the determination of the nature of support of a diocesan priest from a benefice or an office or subsidy.

[68]Cf. *supra*, Chapter IV, Article 2.

[69]"Services" is not a univocal term. Spiritual services can be rendered which are different in kind from temporal services and which are entirely outside the jurisdiction of the State. Cf. D. E. O'Brien, "The First Freedom," *Notre Dame Lawyer*, XXIV (1948), 134-140: *Jural Postulate VIII:* "Ministers of Churches must be able to assume that they may acquire from the members of their Churches voluntary contributions for their decent support under the existing social and economic order, without restriction by the States." A money value can be placed upon temporal services rendered, but in the United States of America, by virtue of the principles of Inter-Church-and-State Common Law and under Amendment I to the Federal Constitution, as applied to the States by the Fourteenth Amendment, no State can exercise jurisdiction over spiritual services to such an extent.

[70]Cf. Ryder, *Simony*, p. 101.

[71]Cf. Richardson, *Just Title*, pp. 18-20; canon 730.

fore, constitute no more than a motive for which an offering is made. They cannot constitute a legally sufficient consideration at American Law, Canon or Secular, sufficient to bring into existence any contract.[72] In the absence of a contract, the money received by a priest from an ecclesiastical pension is not of the nature of compensation.[73]

SEC. 3. IS THE SUPPORT OF DIOCESAN PRIESTS FROM AN ECCLESIASTICAL PENSION OF THE NATURE OF A "GIFT"?

The support which a diocesan priest receives from a subsidy in the form of an ecclesiastical pension in the strict sense, then, inasmuch as it does not come by way of a contractual relationship,[74] must be received by diocesan priests in the United States in the nature of a gift.[75] At Canon Law in the United States the motive for the gift is not pertinent to the nature of the gift.[76] European Canon Law writers, following the civil law of the place in view of the ruling of canon 1529, may and often do speak of such support as a remuneration whose purpose is to support the priest. Remuneration at American Canon Law, in the absence of any special secular legislative provision to the contrary, will be either contractual or non-contractual. Non-contractual sums, under the present legislation, fall into the classification of a "gift." [77] Hence, European writers to the contrary notwithstanding, the support of diocesan priests in the United States from an ecclesiastical pension is of the nature of a gift.

ARTICLE 6. THE NATURE OF SUPPORT OF DIOCESAN PRIESTS UNDER PENAL REMOVAL FROM BENEFICE OR OFFICE

At times a diocesan priest who has been culpably and seriously negligent in his duties is deprived of his benefice or office.[78] The

[72]Cf. Williston, *Contracts*, I, §§ 147-148.

[73]Cf. *supra*, Chapter IV, Art. 2.

[74]*Supra*, Article 5, sec. 2.

[75]*Weagant v. Bowers*, 57 F2d 679 (1932); *Bogardus v. Commissioner of Internal Revenue*, 302 U.S. 34 (1937); cf. *supra*, Chapter IV, Art. 2.

[76]Mertens, *Taxation*, I, p. 249, § 6.08.

[77]Cf. *supra*, Chapter IV.

[78]Penal deprivation of benefice or office differs from mere removal for reasons of ineffectual administration. Cf. canons 2154-2156. The pastor

ordinary has an obligation under the Code of Canon Law to provide support for the diocesan priest under penal removal from office, whether administrative or judicial. Under his title of ordination a diocesan priest has in the matter of his support a right to look to his ordinary, who has the correlative duty to confer upon him a benefice, an office, or a subsidy sufficient for his adequate support.[79] This right is not lost to the priest even upon a penal administrative or judicial removal from or deprivation of office.[80]

There are only two cases in which a diocesan priest loses his right to receive a sufficient support for a decent living: deposition and the perpetual privation of the right to wear the ecclesiastical garb. These two penalties can be inflicted only by means of a due process of Canon Law. By deposition a diocesan priest loses his right to support, but the ordinary is required *in his charity* to provide for the priest in a suitable manner, so that the priest will not be forced, with consequent disgrace to the clerical state, to become a beggar. This obligation on the part of the ordinary is one of Christian charity, and not one of legal justice.[81]

If the deposed priest does not show any signs of amendment, and especially if he continues to give scandal and refuses to heed new warnings, the ordinary is authorized to deprive him perpetually of the right to wear the ecclesiastical garb. A diocesan priest so pun-

---

who is merely removed should be given another benefice, office, or at least an adequate subsidy. Cf. Coronata, *Institutiones,* III, 1593; Wernz-Vidal, *Ius Canonicum,* VI, 761-762.

[79]Cf. canon 981, § 2; Vermeersch-Creusen, *Epitome,* II, 143.

[80]C. Meier, *Penal Administrative Procedure Against Negligent Pastors,* The Catholic University of America Canon Law Studies, n. 140 (Washington, D. C.: The Catholic University of America Press, 1941), p. 215 (hereafter cited *Administrative Procedure);* Schmalzgrueber, *Jus Ecclesiasticum,* Lib. V, tit. 39, n. 305; III Plenary Council of Baltimore, Decree n. 72; S. C. de Prop. Fide, 4 febr. 1873, ad 1—*Collectanea,* n. 1394; *Fontes,* n. 4881.

[81]S. Findlay, *Canonical Norms Governing the Deposition and Degradation of Clerics,* The Catholic University of America Canon Law Studies, n. 130 (Washington, D. C.: The Catholic University of America Press, 1941), pp. 167-171 (hereafter cited as *Deposition and Degradation);* cf. canon 2303, § 2.

ished loses all claim even to a charitable support from the ordinary.[82]

In the case of a diocesan priest who under penal administrative or judicial removal from his benefice or office receives a subsidy through the charity of his ordinary, it cannot be challenged that his subsidy is of the nature of a gift, since it is entirely voluntary on the part of the ordinary, both as to whether it shall be given or not, and also as to the amount that is given. The entire matter is left by the Code of Canon Law to the conscience of the bishop. Any obligations in conscience when absolved through the payment of money, bank checks, or other goods of value, are of the nature of a gift.[83]

In the case of a diocesan priest under penal administrative or judicial removal, the fundamental canon regarding his support is that which requires the ordinary to confer upon all priests ordained on the title of service of the diocese a benefice, an office, or a subsidy sufficient for their adequate support.[84]

If the ordinary confers a benefice upon the penally removed diocesan priest, the nature of support received by the priest will be the same as that which is received by any other priest from a benefice.[85] If the ordinary confers an office upon the priest, the nature of support received by the priest will be the same as that which is received by any other diocesan priest from an ecclesiastical office.[86] If the ordinary confers a subsidy upon the priest, the nature of support received by the priest will be the same as that which is received by any other diocesan priest from a similar subsidy.[87]

---

[82]Findlay, *Deposition and Degradation,* 171-179; cf. canon 2304, § 2.

[83]Cf. *supra,* Chapter IV, Article 2; Williston, *Contracts,* I, § 148.

[84]Canon 981, § 2.

[85]Cf. *supra,* Chapter V, wherein it appears that the support received by a diocesan priest from an ecclesiastical benefice in the United States is of the legal nature of a gift.

[86]Cf. *supra,* Chapter VI, wherein it appears that the support received by a diocesan priest from an ecclesiastical office in the United States is of the legal nature of a gift.

[87]Cf. *supra,* Chapter VII, wherein it appears that the support received by a diocesan priest from an ecclesiastical subsidy in the United States is of the legal nature of a gift.

Chapter VIII

THE NATURE OF SUPPORT OF DIOCESAN PRIESTS IN THE UNITED STATES FROM MASS STIPENDS AND FROM STOLE FEES

In addition to the support received from a benefice, an office, or a subsidy conferred by their ordinary under the prescriptions of the Code of Canon Law, diocesan priests receive a portion of their support from Mass stipends and from stole fees. The legislation of the Code of Canon Law in respect to the support from Mass stipends and stole fees is contained in canons 463, 827-844, 1056, 1234-1237, 1504-1507, 1909, and 2349.[1]

Article 1. The Nature of Support from Mass Stipends

The history of the pre-Code ecclesiastical legislation relative to Mass stipends has been exhaustively covered by many writers.[2] Their unanimous conclusion is that Mass stipends were deemed from the earliest days, and still are so deemed, to be voluntary contributions toward the support of the priest who celebrated and applied the Mass as requested in accordance with the intention of the donor.[3]

---

[1]Cf. Anonymous, "Fees and Stipends," *The Jurist*, I (1941), 335-342.

[2]Among these, see the following Canon Law Studies of the Catholic University of America: C. Keller, *Mass Stipends*, The Catholic University of America Canon Law Studies, n. 27 (Washington, D. C.: The Catholic University of America, 1925); N. Miller, *Founded Masses According to the Code of Canon Law*, The Catholic University of America Canon Law Studies, n. 34 (Washington, D. C.: The Catholic University of America, 1926).

[3]P. Gasparri, *Tractatus Canonicus de Sanctissima Eucharistia* (2 vols., Paris: Delhomme et Briguet, 1897), I, 388 sqq. (hereafter cited as *de Eucharistia);* S. Many, *Praelectiones de Missa* (Paris: Letouzey et Ané, 1903), pp. 76 sqq. hereafter cited as *De Missa);* E. Regatillo, *Ius Sacramentarium* (2 vols., Santander: Sal Terrae, 1945-1946), I, 136 sqq.; Cappello, *De Sacramentis*, I, (4 ed.) 579 sqq.; M. Coronata, *Institutiones Iuris Canonici ad usum utriusque cleri et scholarum: De Sacramentis Tractatus Canonicus*

In the Code of Canon Law, the legislation regarding Mass stipends is contained in canons 827-844. The Code made no legislative changes in the *nature* of support of diocesan priests through Mass stipends, but merely restated the earlier teaching of the Church in this respect. The age-long custom of denominating Mass stipends as *eleemosynae* is continued. *Eleemosynae,* or alms, are without question voluntary contributions.[4]

Commentators on the Code of Canon Law describe Mass stipends as voluntary contributions.[5] It was stated by S. Many (+1922) that according to an established and approved custom of the Church any priest who says and applies a Mass may accept an alms.[6] The practice whereby the faithful were accustomed in the early days of the Church, to offer bread and wine at each Mass they attended and sometimes to lay money upon the altar was universal by the twelfth century.[7] The present day Mass stipend or *eleemosyna* merely takes the place of the offerings which the early Christians were accustomed to give for the support of the priests on the occasion of the celebration of the Mass.[8]

In Mass stipends the money is *not* received *for the Mass* itself, *or for the labor involved* in celebrating and applying the Mass, *or as the price for the Mass,* but only for the support of the priest celebrant.[9] The Mass is freely applied by the priest. The contribution to his support is not the price of the spiritual Mass. The fact of his receiving support is a condition requisite in order that the priest may be able to offer the Mass.[10]

(3 vols., Torino: Marietti, 1943-1946), I, 232 (hereafter cited *De Sacramentis)*; L. Thomassinus, *Vetus et Nova Ecclesiae Disciplina* (Magontiaci, 1787), Pars. III, Lib. I, cap. 7, n. 8; Schmalzgrueber, *Jus Ecclesiasticum,* Lib. III, tit. 30, n. 80.

[4]Cappello, *De Sacramentis,* I, 586; Many, *De Missa,* p. 85; cf. canon 1234, § 1, which identifies the words *taxa* and *eleemosyna* as being of the same voluntary nature.

[5]E.g., cf. Regatillo, *Ius Sacramentarium,* I, 137.

[6]*De Missa,* p. 85.

[7]Many, *De Missa,* pp. 79-83; Regatillo, *Ius Sacramentarium,* I, 137.

[8]Cappello, *De Sacramentis,* I, 582.

[9]Cappello, *De Sacramentis,* I, 584.

[10]Cappello, *De Sacramentis,* I, 584; cf. Gasparri, *De Eucharistia,* I, 388 sqq.

St. Thomas Aquinas (1225-1274), taught the unchanging doctrine of the Catholic Church, namely, that a priest receives a Mass stipend, not as the price for the consecration of the Eucharist, but as a free-will offering for his support.[11] There is a tendency among all the other authors to copy from St. Thomas and from one another.[12]

Canon 824 states that it is lawful for a priest, in accordance with the established and approved custom in the Church, to receive a stipend or *eleemosyna* on the occasion of the celebration of the Mass. Diocesan priests in the United States can turn also to the II Plenary Council of Baltimore, which in 1866 restated the law of the Church on Mass stipends, particularly for this country, in the following words:

> Licite accipi potest stipendium justum seu eleemosyna ad celebrandam Missam, quam quis pro alio celebrare non tenetur; stipendium enim non datur tanquam pretium vel compensatio Missae, sed uti medius ad sustentationem ministri.[13]

It is the undisputed doctrine of the Catholic Church that a priest cannot sell or contract to sell the application of a Mass.[14] To do so would make the priest guilty of the sin and crime of simony.[15] Canon 2371 indicates that a priest who purports to sell his services in the celebration and application of a Mass for any price is suspect of heresy and subject to suspension.

Just as under canon 1529 the Church has adopted as Canon Law certain provisions of the American Secular Law regarding contracts and payments, so under the American Secular Law doctrine of the Conflict of Laws, the American Law adopts *as American*

---

[11]*Summa Theologica,* II-II, q. 100, a. 2, ad 2.

[12]Cf. *supra,* p. 102, note 3, which lists over six authors of world renown and authority, all of whom express similar statements on the matter in nearly identical words.

[13]Decree 369—*Coll. Lac.,* III, 497.

[14]"Sell or contract to sell" are used in the technical meaning of American Canon Law, which is identified by canon 1529 with "sales and contracts to sell" in the American Secular Law.

[15]Many, *De Missa,* p. 88; Cappello, *De Sacramentis,* I, 584; Gasparri *De Eucharistia,* I, 394. The canons relative to simony are 185, 727-730, 1446, 1465, 2371, 2372.

Law certain provisions of Canon Law. On more than one hundred occasions the nature of Mass stipends at American Law has been declared and explained in harmony with their nature at Canon Law. None of these American judicial decisions regarding the nature of Mass stipends has held that the delivery to a priest of a Mass stipend constitutes anything but a gift, and certainly not a contract or a sale.

Since the Code of Canon Law made no changes as affecting the *nature* of Mass stipends, the pre-Code American decisions have equal authority on this matter with those which were decided after the effective date of the Code of Canon Law. All standard case annotators, all standard law digests, all outstanding authors writing on the Common Law, the American Institute in its Restatement of the Law, as well as every American decision in courts of record, unanimously declare that the delivery of a Mass stipend constitutes a gift.[16]

In *Newton v. Carberry*[17] Chief Judge Cranch (1769-1855), speaking for the Circuit Court, District of Columbia, in probably the first truly Mass stipend case in the United States, held bequests for Masses to be of the nature of gifts.

In 1876, in *Schmucker's Estate v. Reel,*[18] the Court held that a bequest for Masses constituted a gift under the American system of law—both canon and secular.[19]

---

[16]Representative of these authorities are: 1) 111 American Law Reports, Annotated, 525 (1937), which classifies all deliveries of Mass stipends as "Gifts for Masses." 2) 11 C.J. 322, which denominates the delivery of Mass stipends to priests as "gifts for the saying of Masses." 3) *Restatement of the Law of Trusts* (2 vols., St. Paul: American Law Institute Publishers, 1935), section 371 g, which treats deliveries of Mass stipends as "gifts." 4) Austin W. Scott in *The Law of Trusts* (4 vols., Boston: Little Brown and Company, 1939) in section 124.4, who does likewise.

[17]5 Cranch C.C. 632 (1840).

[18]61 Mo. 592.

[19]In these and in all other cases the American Courts have recognized, given effect to, and applied the Canon Law regarding Mass stipends as American Law. Since 1918, in regard to contracts and payments, the Church has, in virtue of canon 1529, adopted American Law as Canon Law in the United States. The interplay and influence of the two systems of law upon each other is exemplified in the treatment of Mass stipends.

In the *Estate of Anna Herzo,*[20] Judge Coffey ruled:

> Masses are not bought, any amount or anything given to the priest for their celebration is given as a gratuity or as an alms offering. . . . While the money . . . for Masses is not offered or received as pay for the Masses, it is accepted by the priest and used by him for his support.

Nead's Estate[21] held that the money received by a priest for the celebration and application of a Mass is not compensation but is a gift.[22]

In *O'Donnell's Estate*[23] an attorney for a priest contended that a bequest for Masses was a personal one to the priest as compensation for services to be rendered.[24] The Supreme Court of the State of Pennsylvania held that, at American Law which recognized, gave effect to, and applied Canon Law on the nature of Mass stipends *as American Law,* the contention that the Mass stipend was compensation for services to be rendered could not be sustained because Mass stipends are gifts.

In the *Estate of Reilly*[25] it was urged that Mass stipends were not gifts to priests, but that the money was compensation to them for services to be rendered. The Supreme Court of the State of Ohio, however, ruled as a matter of law that "the money . . . for Masses goes as a gratuity for the personal use of the priest who says the Masses." [26]

---

[20]2 Coffey's Probate Decisions 165 (1902) [California].

[21]55 Penn. Sup'r 573 (1914).

[22]Compare this decision with II Plenary Council of Baltimore, Decree 369—*Coll. Lac.*, III, 497.

[23]209 Pa. 63 (1904).

[24]This contention, made by a secular lawyer in the hope of winning a case, was obviously not the true doctrine of the Church regarding Mass stipends. Cf. Cappello, *De Sacramentis,* I, 584.

[25]138 Ohio State 145 (1941).

[26]Comparison of the language of the Court with Cappello, *De Sacramentis,* I, 584-585, as translated, indicates that the Court recognized, gave effect to, and applied the Canon Law on Mass stipends as the American Law. The Canon Law, by virtue of Canon 1529, recognizes, gives effect to and applies the American Law on payments as Canon Law. Accordingly the nature of Mass stipends will be deemed identical at both systems of law.

Since a Mass stipend is a payment, and the Canon Law and American Law are identical in the matter, it follows that in the United States, as throughout the entire world, Mass stipends are of the nature of a "gift." [27]

ARTICLE 2. THE NATURE OF SUPPORT FROM STOLE FEES

The history of ecclesiastical legislation regarding stole fees has been exhaustively covered by many writers.[28] The unanimous conclusion that stole fees are voluntary contributions *(oblationes vel eleemosynae)* given to priests on the occasion of the administration of the sacraments or the sacramentals is the traditional teaching of the Church.[29] To consider that stole fees are offered as the price of the spiritual benefit involved is entirely contrary to the view of the Church, which considers such an exchange as simony and as forbidden by both divine and ecclesiastical law.[30]

Canon 730 permits the laity to *give* something temporal to the priest on the occasion of the sacred ministry. The canon uses the word *"datur,"* which may mean something given spontaneously, something given at a request, or something given because required.[31] Such a temporal amount transferred to the priest on the occasion of the sacred ministry is called a stole fee. When given spontaneously to the priest a stole fee is obviously of the nature of a gift.[32] When given at a request made of the donor by the priest, then, if the request is not enforceable by the priest at Canon Law, the transfer is likewise of the nature of a gift.[33]

---

[27] Cf. Appendix, *infra*, pp. 129 ff., for an exhaustive list of all reported cases in American Courts of record regarding Mass stipends. The case of *Ross v. City of Philadelphia* (25 Atl. 2d 834), omitted here, will be treated hereafter.

[28] Among the many, cf. W. Ferry, *Stole Fees*, The Catholic University of America Canon Law Studies, n. 59 (Washington, D. C.: The Catholic University of America, 1930).

[29] Blat, *Commentarium*, III, 11; Cance, *Le Code*, II, 203; Coronata, *Institutiones*, II, 17; Cappello, *De Sacramentis*, I, 71-73; Vermeersch-Creusen, *Epitome*, II, 5; Richardson, *Just Title*, pp. 17-19; Ferry, *Stole Fees*, p. 2; Ryder, *Simony*, p. 101.

[30] Blat, *Commentarium*, III, 11; Richardson, *Just Title*, p. 19.

[31] Richardson, *Just Title*, p. 18.

[32] Cf. *supra*, Chapter IV, Article 3.

[33] Cf. *supra*, Chapter IV, Article 3.

Regarding stole fees given because required by the priest, canon 736 expressly forbids priests to exact anything on the occasion of the sacred ministry except the offerings that are allowed in canon 1507. Canon 2408 makes the violation of canon 1507 a delict to which grave penalties are attached. Under the provisions of canon 1507 it is the right of a provincial council to determine the *taxa* or *eleemosyna*[34] to be given on the occasion of the administration of the sacraments and local ordinaries generally have no power to determine stole fees for their own dioceses, except as to Mass stipends and offerings on the occasion of funerals.[35] Furthermore, any schedule of *taxae* or offerings the amount of which is determined by legislation of a provincial council, must be approved by the Holy See before it is of any force or effect.[36]

In those provinces in which there has been made no such determination by a provincial council, and even in those in which there has been such a determination but prior to the approval thereof by the Holy See, the priest is permitted by Canon Law, under penalty of committing a delict, to receive absolutely nothing except the entirely voluntary gifts of the faithful.[37] If a diocesan priest demands anything more than whatever amount is approved by the Holy See after enactment by a provincial council the doctors disagree whether he should be deemed guilty of simony or not.[38] Ryder, with others, asserts that, regardless of the situation in the internal forum of conscience, any external violation of this law constitutes at least a strong presumption of simony in the external forum of Canon Law. The person from whom a priest demands

---

[34]The amount of the offering which may be required is called at Canon Law a *"taxa"*, and is of the identical nature as *"eleemosyna"*, which is voluntary gift. Cf. canon 1234; *supra*, p. 103.

[35]Cf. canons 831 and 1234; cf. S. C. C., *Dioecesis M. et. Aliarum*, 11 dec. 1920—*AAS*, XIII (1921), 315.

[36]Canon 1507; Cf. canons 250, § 2; 291, § 1; S. C. Consist., 21 apr. 1910, *AAS*—II (1910), 329-330.

[37]Cappello, *De Sacramentis*, I, 72. Cf. canons 736, 2408, 463 § 1. The amount of this gift may be determined by approved custom, but it may not be exacted.

[38]Cf. Vermeersch-Creusen, *Epitome*, II, 7; Richardson, *Just Title*, pp. 53-54. Canon 463, § 2, definitely establishes the guilt of injustice in such a case.

anything in excess of what is authorized may denounce the priest to the ordinary as allegedly guilty of a delict under canon 2408, and the priest may be coerced by means of a judicial action to make restitution of any amount which he may have taken in violation of the law of the Church.[39]

It is a question of fact in each ecclesiastical province of the United States whether a provincial council has set up a list of stole fees in the amount in which a priest may ask for them, and also a question of fact whether such a list, if any there be, has been approved by the Holy See. Even when in fact such a list has been both enacted and approved, the priest has but a limited right to demand the specified stole fee. Canon 463, § 4, requires the pastor to exercise his sacred ministry gratuitously in the case of those persons who are not financially able to make an offering in the amount approved by the Holy See upon the enactment of the provincial council. In the event that a person is capable of making the specified offering, that person remains free either to make the offering or to refuse it. In the case of a deliberate refusal such a person may be guilty of a delict under canon 2349. The priest is given under Canon Law no direct power of action to enforce the making of the offering. He can merely denounce the recusant to the ordinary as allegedly guilty of a delict under canon 2349, which reserves the right and the power to enforce the making of the offering *(praestatio)* to the ordinary, who in his prudent judgment is authorized to punish the recusant until he has satisfied the legitimate demand of the Church.

In a not inconsiderable number of ecclesiastical provinces in the United States no list of stole fees has been enacted and approved. In such provinces in the absence of any approved custom which has fixed a traditional fee, the priest can accept only the voluntary and spontaneous gifts of the faithful on the occasion of the sacred ministry. Otherwise he appears to commit the delict which according to the wording of canon 2408 warrants the imposition of a heavy pecuniary fine.[40] The priests in these provinces wherein there

[39]Canons 463, § 2; 2408. Cf. Ryder, *Simony,* pp. 106-107; Richardson, *Just Title,* pp. 53-54.

[40]The only province with such a list approved by the Holy See, as far as is known to the writer, is the Province of Portland in Oregon, which

is not extant any schedule approved by the Holy See are required; in the absence of any and every regulative approved custom, freely to give of spiritual things placed in their charge and the faithful are invited freely to give on the occasion of the sacred ministry some temporal amount for the support of the priest.[41]

This is the fundamental explanation of the nature of taxes, stole fees, voluntary offerings, collections, stipends, etc., as related to the sacraments, the Mass, preaching, catechizing, and other uses of the power of orders and/or of jurisdiction. In the United States their nature constitutes them all, at Canon and Secular Law alike, as voluntary gifts.[42] The fact that the amount of the stole fee or the stipend is sometimes denominated as a tax[43] does not change the nature of the transaction. Once the voluntary nature of the transaction has been seen, it is sufficient to point out that every tax is not a price, since taxing is merely defining and determining some set contribution.[44] Hence a voluntary gift made in a determined amount as affording a means of sustenance may be called a tax.[45]

A gift does not cease to remain a gift simply for the reason that the law of a provincial council, or any other legislation, has decreed the amount in which the gift should be made.[46] A gift is still a gift

---

enacted this legislation in 1932. The Synodal Statutes of the Diocese of Toledo, Ohio, are exemplary of the situation in most of the archdioceses and dioceses of the United States: "No fee may be exacted for the administration of any Sacrament. Stole fees are not exactions but gratuities regulated by the Church."—*Acta et Decreta Synodi Dioecesanae Toletanae Primae* (Toleti: Cancelleria Curiae Dioecesanae, 1941), n. 393. Cf. *supra,* note 35. Cf. F. Murphy, *Legislative Powers of the Provincial Council,* The Catholic University of America Canon Law Studies, n. 257 (Washington, D. C.: The Catholic University of America Press, 1947), pp. 58-60; cf. Richardson, *Just Title,* p. 54.

[41]Cf. Matt., X, 8. Cf. canons 736; 463; 2408.

[42]Cf. Richardson, *Just Title,* p. x.

[43]Cf. canon 1507.

[44]Cf. Richardson, *Just Title,* 6. 48.

[45]"Tax" is not a univocal word, and its meaning at Canon Law is definitely different from its technical meaning at American Secular Law. Cf. Coronata, *Institutiones,* II, 124; D'Angelo, *Tasse e Pensioni,* p. 9.

[46]Cf. Richardson, *Just Title,* p. 48. Canon 1234 identifies *taxa* and *eleemosyna* as being of the same nature. Alike, they are of the nature of a gift.

even though the amount be determined by some one other than the donor. A man may make a gift, for example, to a Symphony Association or an Opera Reading Club, of $5.00 to be an "active" member. If he wishes to be a "supporting" member, then under the rules and regulations of the Association or Club he will make a gift of $25.00. Such a transaction is admittedly a charitable gift. In either case the man is free with a freedom that allows him to select between contradictories, to give or not to give, and this is precisely the freedom that underlies either the essence and the nature of a gift, even though for incidental reasons the amount which he gives is not controlled by his own choice but is specified at the wish of another.[47] Under the Code of Canon Law, which made no legislative changes regarding the *nature* of stole fees, the pre-Code doctrine of the Catholic Church that stole fees are offerings made to a priest on the occasion of the administration of the sacraments and the sacramentals is still the pertinent and applicable doctrine of the Church.[48]

Only one case involving stole fees has been found in the secular courts of the United States.[49] This is the case of *Ross v. City of Philadelphia, et al.*,[50] in which the Pennsylvania Superior Court ruled, as matter of law, on a demurrer, that stole fees are not received as contractual compensation, but as gifts, because under the rules, regulations, canons, faith and discipline of the Roman Catholic Church offerings of money and other articles of value received from individuals at whose request marriages, baptisms, and other religious services are performed by priests, are voluntary contributions, unenforceable by virtue of any contractual relationship, liability, or responsibility, and Catholic priests are prohibited from

---

[47]Cf. K. O'Brien, "Replication," *The Jurist*, III (1943), 452, ff.

[48]Ferry, *Stole Fees*, pp. 2, 10-11; Ryder, *Simony*, p. 101; Richardson, *Just Title*, pp. 17-19; Coronata, *Institutiones*, II, 17; Cappello, *De Sacramentis*, I, 71-73; Cance, *Le Code*, II, 203; Blat, *Commentarium*, III, 11; Vermeersch-Creusen, *Epitome*, II, 5.

[49]Note that Regatillo in treating of stole fees in Spain repeatedly cites the civil law from the Spanish Civil Code.—*Institutiones*, I, 43.

[50]25 Atl. 2d 834 (1942); treated more fully by O'Brien in "The Parish Priest and the Federal Income Tax Under the Revenue Act of 1942," *The Jurist*, III (1943) 129 ff.

demanding, or exacting a fee, price, or consideration of any character for such services. The offerings which a priest receives by virtue of his priesthood on the occasion of the sacred ministry are pure gratuities, which the priest has no right to demand, but which he is permitted to receive when they are tendered.

Thus, under both the American Canon Law and the American Secular Law, there is no recognition of any contractual compensation in the case of stole fees. They are, accordingly, of the legal nature of a "gift."

CHAPTER IX

THE NATURE OF SUPPORT OF DIOCESAN PRIESTS FROM OTHER THAN HEREINABOVE SOURCES

In addition to the support received from the above mentioned ecclesiastical sources—the support as regulated within the exclusive jurisdiction of the Church and subject to Canon Law in view of its essential nature—diocesan priests in the United States may lawfully, and at times actually do, receive support from other than these sources. This is entirely within the rights of diocesan priests at both Canon Law[1] and American Law.[2]

Support received by a diocesan priest from sources other than an ecclesiastical benefice, office, subsidy, Mass stipends or stole fees, is frequently received by him, not as a priest but rather as any other individual person receives it, and hence it is received outside the scope of the jurisdiction of the Church. Support received outside the jurisdiction of the Church is a temporal matter which relative to its nature is within the exclusive jurisdiction of the State.[3]

As examples of support received from such sources by diocesan priests, which examples are not meant to be recounted all-inclusively here, one may list the following: dividends; interest; annuities; pensions; rents; gains from the sale or exchange of property; profits from investments; wages; salaries of teachers in universities or colleges, as a general rule; compensation from the Federal government, from state, city or county governments, or from Federal

[1]Certain restrictions, however, are placed upon diocesan priests in that canons 139 and 142 prescribe some non-ecclesiastical sources for such additional support. Cf. Brunini, *Clerical Obligations, passim.*

[2]There are placed upon diocesan priests only such restrictions as are placed also upon other citizens, since no special treatment, whether preferential or discriminatory, is accorded to the question of the support of diocesan priests as such under American Law.

[3]Cf. D. O'Brien, "The First Freedom," *Notre Dame Lawyer,* XXIV, (1948), 134-140.

agencies for services rendered by the priest as a citizen or as a public officer rather than as a member of the clergy; the compensation of military chaplains in the armed forces; royalties on inventions, copyrights, mineral leases, art works, writings; and so on. In substance, such support is received by diocesan priests as American citizens in the same manner as similar support is received by any other citizen—subject exclusively to the secular laws in the United States of America as to its nature. No special treatment, whether preferential or discriminatory, is accorded to the question of this support at American Law when the support is incidentally received by a priest the while the law completely abstracts from his priestly condition and status.

Since the determination of the nature of this kind of support is a temporal matter outside the scope of the Canon Law, no further treatment will herein be given to the nature of this support received by diocesan priests from sources other than those subject to the norms of Canon Law. It may safely be stated, however, without the slightest fear of contradiction, that if under the laws of the United States such support is of the nature of compensation when it is received by a lay citizen, it is also of the nature of compensation when under identical circumstances it is received by a diocesan priest. If, moreover, this support is of the nature of a gift when received by a lay citizen, it is likewise of the nature of a gift when under identical circumstances it is received by a diocesan priest.

Chapter X

SOME LEGAL EFFECTS IN SECULAR LAW OF THE NATURE OF SUPPORT OF DIOCESAN PRIESTS

Article 1. The Diocesan Priest and the Income Tax

In the United States a tax is placed by the Internal Revenue Code upon "income."[1] Income, however, is not a univocal word. The meaning of the term income as used in the Internal Revenue Code and in common conversation is not the same.[2] Taxable income, although allied to economic income, is statutory and not necessarily actual income.[3]

Many meanings of the term income are found in common usage. To ascertain exactly the meaning of "income" as used in the Internal Revenue Code is not essential to the purposes of this study, for there has been adopted by the Internal Revenue Code as an antithesis of income the classification of "gift." All money, bank checks, or other goods of value, received by a diocesan priest for his support must fall either within the classification of "income" or the classification of "gift."[4] The statute specifically provides that gifts shall not be included in gross income and shall be exempt from income tax.[5]

Gross income from which the tax is calculated includes "gains, profits, and income derived from salaries, wages or compensation for personal services . . . of whatever kind and in whatever form paid, or from professions, vocations, trades, businesses, commerce

[1]The Internal Revenue Code is Title 26 of the United States Code. 26 U.S.C. § 22(a).

[2]Cf. Mertens, *Taxation*, I, § 1.10.

[3]Mertens, *Taxation*, I, § 1.10.

[4]Cf. *Bogardus v. Commissioner of Internal Revenue*, 302 U. S. 34 (1937). The classification of "capital gains" is not herein considered, since the support of priests from ecclesiastical sources does not involve such items.

[5]26 U.S.C. § 22(b) (3).

or sales . . . also from . . . the transaction of business carried on for gain or profit."[6]

It is to be noted that the activities of diocesan priests as such are performed not for temporal gain but for the promotion of divine worship and the salvation of souls. The temporal support received is not of the nature of temporal gain, but it is only an equitable and suitable support which is accessory to the spiritual nature of their activities and therefore of the same spiritual nature.[7]

Sec. 1. Support from Benefice, Office, or Subsidy

The Internal Revenue Code decrees that money received as salary, wages, or compensation for personal services is taxable income. Money, whether in the form of cash or bank checks, received by a diocesan priest in the United States from his ecclesiastical benefice, office, or subsidy for his support is, in common conversation, frequently called the priest's "salary." [8]

---

[6] 26 U.S.C. § 22(a).

[7] Schmalzgrueber, *Jus Ecclesiasticum,* Lib. V, tit. 49, n. 10.

[8] "Salary" is an approximate transliteration, or perhaps a slavish translation of the Latin word *"salarium,"* which was first applied to the support of diocesan priests in the United States by the III Plenary Council of Baltimore (Decree 273), at which time it was given a technical legal meaning at Canon Law as identical with *"congrua"*—a portion of the gifts of the faithful which is applied for the support of the priest. The transliteration of *"salarium"* (a term having a distinct technical meaning at Canon Law) from Latin into English, involving in this process the use of the word "salary" (a term having an equally distinct though different technical meaning at both English and American Law), has led to confusion regarding the taxability of support received by a priest. Since "salary" connotes a Common Law contract of employment, it has been inferred by some that priests receive support from a contract of employment. This inference is not warranted at law, simply in view of the conversational misuse of the technical legal term "salary." Cf. *supra,* Chapter II, p. 18. As to the use of the word "salary" not involving any contractual relationship in the case of Methodist Episcopal clergymen, cf. *"Hearings Relative to the Social Security Act Amendments of 1939 before the Committee on Ways and Means, House of Representatives, Seventy-Sixth Congress, First Session* (revised print, Washington, D. C.: U. S. Government Printing Office, 1939), pp. 2107-2108 (hereafter cited as *Hearings, Ways and Means, 1939).* The case of *Schall v. Commissioner of Internal Revenue,* decided by the

As used in the Internal Revenue Code the phrase "salary, wages or compensation for personal services" implies a contract of employment.[9] It imports a specific contract for a specific sum for a certain period of time.[10] Further it is said to have four characteristics—first, that it is paid for temporal services rendered; secondly, that it is paid under some contract; thirdly, that it is computed by time; and fourthly, that it is payable at a fixed time.[11] In every case involving salary, as that term is used in the Internal Revenue Code, there must be, of its essence, an existent contract under which the salary is paid.

There is no contract at Canon Law, or at American Law which on this point is identical with Canon Law, whereby a priest receives his "salary" whether from a benefice,[12] an office,[13] or a subsidy.[14] The support received by a diocesan priest from these ecclesiastical sources, although called his "salary,"[15] is at law in the United States of the nature of a "gift."[16]

The United States Supreme Court has declared the following as the law of the land:

> If the sum of money under consideration . . . [is] . . . a gift and not compensation, it is exempt from [income] taxa-

Tax Court of the United States (11 T.C. No. 16, July 30, 1948) establishes the importance of distinguishing the legal relation between the Catholic priest and his congregation in the United States from the legal relations between ministers of other churches and their congregations, just as the legal relations between the minister and the congregations of every other denomination have to be distinguished from one another in American civil church law. Cf. Zollmann, *American Church Law,* 349, 350.

9*Davis v. Fall River,* 155 Mass. 96, 29 N.E. 202. Cf. *Railway Clearing House v. Druce,* 42 T. L. R. 663, 664 ("connotes contractually secured payment.").

10*Blick v. Mercantile Trust, etc., Co.,* 113 Md. 494.

11Cf. 54 C. J. 1124-1125.

12*Supra,* Chapter V.

13*Supra,* Chapter VI.

14*Supra,* Chapter VII.

15Cf. *Hearings, Ways and Means, 1939,* pp. 2107-2108, as to similar use of the term "salary" to denote non-contractual voluntary gifts received by Methodist Episcopal clergymen for their support.

16*Supra,* Chapters V, VI, VII.

tion and cannot be made taxable by resort to any form of subclassification. If it be in fact a gift, that is an end of the matter; and inquiry as to whether it is a gift of one sort or another is irrelevant. This is necessarily true, for since all gifts are made non-taxable [under the Income Tax sections of the Internal Revenue Code] there can be no such thing under the statute as a taxable gift. . . .[17]

It follows that no diocesan priest is under any duty to report his so-called salary from an ecclesiastical benefice, office, or subsidy as subject to the income tax.[18] A priest in taking this position and not reporting his "salary" from these sources as subject to an income tax is not evading his obligation to support the state. "The law expects you to pay your correct tax—no more—no less. . . . Exempt income should be omitted from your return altogether."[19]

The contrary position, namely that which suggests reporting support which is of the legal nature of a gift at both Canon Law and American Secular Law as if it were a contractual compensation legally enforceable at American Secular Law, could be considered by some as reflecting a disbelief of the priest in the canonical doctrine of the Catholic Church in respect to the nature of the support of a diocesan priest, and thus interpreted by them could insinuate that the received support involves simony at the Divine Law.[20]

---

[17]*Bogardus v. Commissioner of Internal Revenue,* 302 U.S. 34 (1937), 82 L. ed. 32.

[18]Cf. K. O'Brien, "The Parish Priest and the Federal Income Tax under the Revenue Act of 1942," *The Jurist,* III (1943), 129 ff. In recent years it has been the practice of many diocesan priests in the United States to declare as taxable, in their Income Tax returns, the monthly amounts which they receive for their support from church funds, which sums admittedly are usually called "salary" (though with a technical canonical meaning which differs from the usage of the word at American Law). It is submitted, however, that no Catholic writer of any standing has advocated the soundness of this practice either on theological or on legal grounds.

[19]U. S. Government, Treasury Department, Bureau of Internal Revenue, *Official Instructions, How to Prepare your U.S. Income Tax Return on Form 1040 for 1948* (Washington: U. S. Government Printing Office, 1948), pp. 2 and 5.

[20]The collecting of the income tax by means of deducting the amount of the tax from wages and other remuneration from employment at the time

SEC. 2. SUPPORT FROM MASS STIPENDS AND STOLE FEES

The United States Treasury Department, Bureau of Internal Revenue, has issued regulations which state that:

> "marriage fees, baptismal offerings, sums paid for saying masses for the dead, and other contributions received by a clergyman, evangelist, or religious worker for services rendered"

are to be deemed "Compensation for Personal Services," and consequently are subject to the Federal Income Tax.[21] *THIS REGULATION HAS NEVER BEEN UPHELD IN ANY JUDICIAL DECISION!!!*[22]

In the only case in any court of record in which it was brought up for judicial consideration it was declared to be without force.[23] In this connection a statement of the United States Supreme Court is of importance:

---

such money is paid is required of employers under 26 U.S.C. § 1401. It follows from the voluntary nature of the support of diocesan priests from an ecclesiastical benefice, office, or subsidy, that inasmuch as it is of the nature of a gift, neither the bishop, the pastor, the parishioners, or anyone else, is under any duty, or has the right, to deduct or withhold any amount as income tax from any monthly payments received from a benefice, office, or subsidy, by the priests for their support, and to pay the same into the United States Treasury.

The practice of certain Chancery Offices of reporting to the Collector of Internal Revenue on Form No. 1099 (and transmittal Form No. 1096) as "compensation" the total amount of the so-called "salary" of priests attached to the staff of the diocesan curia is likewise contrary to the true doctrine of the nature of the support of such priests, which is that of a "gift" at both Canon and American Secular Law, and may on the part of those who espouse a strict legal viewpoint in the matter be interpreted as implying that the priests or the Curia involved are guilty of simony forbidden by the Divine Law.

[21] 26 CFR, Cum, Supp. § 29.22(a)2. This regulation has been adopted verbatim in the regulations of several State and Municipal Income Tax jurisdictions.

[22] *Ross v. City of Philadelphia and the Receiver of Taxes,* 25 Atl. 2d 834 (1942); cf. Mertens, *Taxation,* I, § 8.04.

[23] *Supra, Ross v. City of Philadelphia, etc.*

"Treasury regulations can add nothing to income as defined by Congress."[24]

The canonical doctrine of the Catholic Church regarding the nature of Mass stipends and stole fees is that they are of the nature of a "gift."[25] This doctrine was recognized, given effect and applied because of rules of pleading in the Ross case, the only judicial decision on the question in American secular courts, in which case it was held that stipends for Masses, and offerings on the occasion of marriages, baptisms, and funerals as received by diocesan priests in the United States are not income but are gifts.[26]

Since, under the Internal Revenue Code as interpreted by the United States Supreme Court,[27] there is "no such thing under the [income tax] statute as a taxable gift," it follows that no priest is under obligation to report support from Mass stipends and stole fees as subject to the Income Tax.[28]

Sec. 3. Support from Other Than Ecclesiastical Sources

Some diocesan priests do in fact receive money from other than the above discussed sources. Such other sources may consist among others of savings bank interest, stock dividends, bond interest, rents and royalties, capital gains on the sale and exchange of property. Such support is not received from ecclesiastical sources.[29] Such support is temporal in its source and hence its nature is not subject to the exclusive jurisdiction of the Church.

---

[24] *M. E. Blatt Co. v. United States,* 305 U.S. 267, 83 L.ed. 187 (1938); cf. *Manhattan General Equipment Co. v. Commissioner of Internal Revenue,* 297 U.S. 129, 80 L.ed. 528 (1936).

[25] *Supra,* Chapter VIII.

[26] Cf. *supra,* Chapter VIII. Cf. *Ross v. City of Philadelphia* 25 Atl. 2d 834 (1942). Other cases turning solely on the nature of Mass stipends are listed in the Appendix.

[27] *Bogardus v. Commissioner of Internal Revenue,* 302 U.S. 34.

[28] Cf. O'Brien, "The Parish Priest and the Federal Income Tax under the Revenue Act of 1942," *The Jurist,* III (1943), 129 ff.

[29] Support received under a contract from certain Catholic corporations as a university or a college by diocesan priests who are acting as proctors, instructors, teachers, or administrative officers, is, in the opinion of the writer, to be included herein.

Such money is of exactly the same nature as similar receipts accruing to any other citizen of the United States. No special treatment, whether preferential or discriminatory, is to be accorded to the question of such income on the score simply that the recipient happens to be a diocesan priest. Such money is subject to taxation on the exact terms of the Internal Revenue Code and any other Titles of the United States Code which may be applicable. If it be in fact income, it is subject to the Income Tax and *must* be reported as such by the diocesan priest, who is obliged, say some, to pay the tax thereon under pain of actual sin. If, however, it be in fact a gift, it need not be reported as income,[30] but may be reported in accordance with the provisions of the Gift Tax Law.

It is respectfully submitted that diocesan priests should be most exact in reporting as subject to the income tax any such taxable income they may receive. This is of prime importance, particularly in view of the delicate situation in which the Catholic Church in the United States is placed at the present time, when agitation on the part of certain citizens is tending to the withdrawal of all real estate tax exemptions enjoyed by the Church. It is respectfully suggested with equal emphasis that diocesan priests should be most exact in *not* reporting as subject to the income tax any non-taxable support which they receive as gifts. This is of prime importance, lest enemies of the Church should apply secular legal principles to this action and conclude that, as a matter of law, Catholics in the United States are buying and selling the sacraments and sacramentals.

Article 2. The Diocesan Priest and the Federal Social Security Laws

Attempts have been made to include diocesan priests under the Federal Social Security Act, as amended.[31] The Federal Social Security Act, as amended, provides, among other things, for old

[30]*Official Instructions, How to Prepare your U.S. Income Tax Return on Form 1040 for 1948*, p. 5.

[31]*Hearings, Ways and Means, 1939*, pp. 2106-2109. *Hearings before the Committee on Finance, United States Senate, Seventy-Sixth Congress, First Session, on HR 6635* (revised print, Washington: United States Government

age benefits.[32] All employers of one or more persons for any period of time, however short, in non-exempt employment are subject to the law and liable for old age benefit taxes.[33] Employers who do not fall within the classification of those bound by the present statute may *NOT* voluntarily subject themselves thereunto. There is no authority under the present act for the collecting of taxes from persons or organizations if they are excepted from the taxing provisions of the act.[34]

In addition to other taxes, such as the income tax and the Workmen's Compensation Insurance Tax, employees are made subject to a Federal Social Security tax upon the income which they receive from their employment.[35] The Common Law employer-employee relationship must exist between the employer and the individuals engaged by him if the employer is to be held liable for such taxes upon their wages.[36] The tax imposed is to be withheld from the wages and collected by the employer from the taxpayer by deducting the amount of the tax from the wages when paid.[37] Certain employment is exempt by statute.[38] Service performed in the employ of a corporation, fund, or foundation organized and operated exclusively for religious, charitable, scientific, literary, or

---

Printing Office, 1939), pp. 363 ff., at p. 365, and p. 463 (hereafter cited as *Hearings, Finance, 1939).* In the 80th Congress (1946-1948) four bills were introduced, all of which provided a foundation for the legal conclusion that diocesan priests were to be made subject to the Social Security Act. According to The New York Times, Friday, December 3, 1948, p. 19, an amendment to the Social Security Act to be proposed at the First Session of the 81st Congress is intended to call for coverage of the lay and ordained workers in churches.

[32] 42 U.S.C. Chapter 7.

[33] 42 U.S.C. § 1004.

[34] 26 U.S.C. § 1421. Cf. Treasury Department, Internal Revenue Bureau, 1937 Rulings, n. 1,394.

[35] 42 U.S.C. § 1001.

[36] 42 U.S.C. § 1011; 20 CFR, Cum. Supp., § 403.804.

[37] 42 U.S.C. § 1002.

[38] 42 U.S.C. § 1011.

educational purposes, is expressly exempt from the present provisions of the Social Security Act, as amended.[39]

In the year 1939 an attempt expressly to include diocesan priests under the old age benefit sections of the act was made in Congress through the introduction of several Bills providing that the exemption of religious societies from the scope of the Federal Social Security Act, as amended, be ended, and that all employees of religious societies be included within the provisions of the Act.[40] This attempt was opposed by the Administrative Board of Bishops of the National Catholic Welfare Conference in the Congressional hearings on the matter.[41]

To be subject to the present provisions of the Act, as amended, it is essential that the Common Law employer-employee relationship *de facto* exist.[42] In the case of diocesan priests receiving support from an ecclesiastical benefice, office, or subsidy, the employer-employee relationship does not exist.[43] Since an essential requisite is missing in the case of diocesan priests, it follows that they cannot lawfully, under the present statute, be subject to any provisions of the Federal Social Security Act, as amended, even though the

[39]42 U.S.C. § 1011. Cf. *supra,* note 31, regarding proposed legislation affecting this exemption. H.R. 447, 81st Congress, 1st Session, is a Bill introduced to extend the coverage of the Social Security Act to include, under a waiver of exemption, the employees of non-profit institutions. Other Bills have also been introduced for the purpose of altering the legislation.

[40]It was mistakenly thought by certain individuals that diocesan priests are employees. This position is without sound legal foundation. Cf. *supra,* Chapters IV, V, VI, VII, VIII. Cf. *Hearings, Finance, 1939,* pp. 363 sqq.

[41]"The administrative board of bishops is desirous of gaining for the lay workers in Catholic institutions the benefits which accrue to employees generally under the Social Security Act . . . The administrative board recommends . . . that the clergy . . . be not included in the category of employees . . ."—*Hearings, Finance, 1939,* p. 364.

[42]42 U.S.C. § 1011; 20 CFR, Cum. Supp., § 403.804.

[43]Cf. *supra,* Chapters V, VI, and VII. Cf. the masterly presentation in the House of Representatives Hearings on behalf of the Methodist Episcopal ministers to the effect that the legal relationship of employer-employee does not exist in their case, and that although their support is called a "salary" it is in reality a voluntary gift.—*Hearings, Ways and Means, 1939,* pp. 2108-2109.

priest or his bishop might wish voluntarily to enter into the plan.[44]

No worthwhile purpose is served by any attempts to include diocesan priests under the Federal Social Security Act. The Catholic Church, under its own organic law, provides for the adequate support of diocesan priests, through all the eventualities of life, in sickness and in health, until death.[45] It is submitted, moreover, that the support of diocesan priests through all said eventualities of life is a temporal matter so annexed to the spiritual that it falls within the exclusive jurisdiction of the Church.[46] Voluntarily to yield jurisdiction over a spiritual matter to the State is beyond the scope of the authority of the clergy in the United States of America.[47]

Article 3. The Diocesan Priest and the Workmen's Compensation Laws

In one or more of the dioceses of the United States, Workmen's Compensation Insurance has been taken out on diocesan priests.[48] Workmen's Compensation Insurance now prevails in all 48 states and in six additional American territories. It affects directly or indirectly the rights at American Secular Law of about 46,000,000 workers annually.[49]

The various statutes which are known as Workmen's Compensa-

---

[44]Cf. *supra,* note 34. The only manner in which diocesan priests could be made subject to the provisions of Social Security is by an amendment to the Act which would permit either of two situations: 1) that those who are not within the employer-employee relationship come *voluntarily* into the plan; Cf. *In re Employment of Church of England Curates* [1912] 2 Ch. 563, in which although the employer-employee relationship did not in fact exist the curates were permitted in England voluntarily to come under a Workmen's Compensation Insurance plan; or 2) that those who are supported by voluntary gifts must, under compulsion, enter into the plan as well as employees.

[45]Canon 981, § 2; III Plenary Council of Baltimore, Decrees 70-73 incl.; cf. also the various diocesan statutes on the same subject in their local implementation of this legislation.

[46]Cf. Schmalzgrueber, *Jus Ecclesiasticum,* Lib. V, tit. 47, n. 10.

[47]Canons 336, 220.

[48]This fact has been communicated privately to the writer by the secretaries of the ordinaries.

[49]Cf. Horovitz, "Current Trends in Basic Principles of Workmen's Compensation," *The Law Society Journal,* XII (1947), 465.

tion Acts, while alike in the object they seek to attain, are so numerous that any analysis of them here must be, of necessity, general in its terms. However, a Workmen's Compensation Act may be broadly defined as a statute providing that in the case of an injury to an employee, when the employment, the employee, and the injury are within the operation of the act, the injured employee or his dependents shall be paid an amount to be determined in accordance with a fixed system or schedule.[50]

Compensation[51] and the right thereto[52] have been held to be based solely on the fact of employment, the liability likewise arising out of the relationship of employer and employee.[53] The rights and duties of the respective parties under Workmen's Compensation Acts have been said to arise out of, and to be incidental to, the contract of employment.[54] To be within the legal scope of any Workmen's Compensation Act, the relationship of employer and employee, in the sense of this relation at Common Law, must exist. Since this relation is contractual in character, it is of the essence of any right deriving from such an Act that a contract of employment actually exist.[55] Moreover, this contract of employment, hire, or service, must be legal or lawful and valid.[56] In the absence of such a contract between the parties there is no legal remedy whereby, in the case of injury, a person may claim and obtain relief under a Workmen's Compensation Act.[57]

---

[50] 71 C. J. 225.

[51] *Hoehn v. Schenck,* 223 N.Y.S. 418.

[52] *McDonough v. National Hospital Ass'n,* 294 P. 351.

[53] *Cudahy Packing Co. v. Parramore,* 263 U.S. 418, 68 L. ed. 366.

[54] Cf. 71 C. J. 239.

[55] 71 C. J. 418, and 428.

[56] 71 C. J. 432.

[57] It is submitted that the inclusion of diocesan priests under Workmen's Compensation Insurance is frequently urged, with some success, by insurance salesmen who are desirous of increasing their own commissions through the sale of such insurance, even though the priest could not legally collect thereunder, and the suit to enforce the collection might result merely in a refund of the premium.

Diocesan priests in the United States receive cash or bank checks from their ecclesiastical benefice, office, or subsidy under no contract of employment or any other type of contract at law—whether Canon Law or American Law.[58] The inclusion of diocesan priests in any plan of Workmen's Compensation Insurance does violence to the Canon Law nature of the support of diocesan priests, and might be interpreted as involving such priests in a violation of the canons of the Code in which simony is proscribed.[59]

---

[58]No reported cases in the American secular courts have been found regarding the awarding of Workmen's Compensation to diocesan priests. Under the British National Insurance Act of 1911 it was determined that curates or assistant curates in the Church of England are not persons employed under any contract of service; *In re Employment of Church of England Curates* [1912] 2 Ch. 563, 6 B.W.C.C. No. 3. Ministers of the United Methodist Church and ministers under probation of the Wesleyan Methodist Church are likewise not employed under any contract; *Re Employment of Ministers of United Methodist Church,* 6 B.W.C.C. No. 1. Methodist Episcopal ministers in the United States are not employees and are supported not through any contractual relationship whatsoever, even though their support is called "salary;" *Hearings, Ways and Means,* 1939, pp. 2107-2108.

[59]Those few diocesan priests who are receiving their support from sources other than an ecclesiastical benefice, office, or subsidy, that is, under a contract of employment, e.g., the priests who are imitating a recent European practice by working in factories in order that they may more readily reach and teach the working classes, or who are under contract to a college or a university, or under any other contract by which they are supported, are in exactly the same legal situation as any layman in the same circumstances. Such priests may well be brought within the legal scope of Workmen's Compensation Acts regarding employment as based on such contractual arrangements. It is to be noted, however, that they do not receive such support as diocesan priests. Rather, if it is received at all, it is due them in view of the activities which they perform as individual citizens.

FINDINGS OF FACT AND CONCLUSIONS OF LAW

I

Findings of Fact

1. Priests in the primitive Church were supported by the voluntary contributions (i.e., the alms) of the faithful.

2. Diocesan priests in the United States are supported by the voluntary contributions (i.e., the alms) of the faithful in the same manner as the priests in the primitive Church.

3. The quantum of support received by priests in the primitive Church was determined, in some instances, by their bishop in accordance with the zeal of the priests in fulfilling their religious duties.

4. The quantum of support received by diocesan priests in the United States is determined by their bishop.

5. Diocesan priests in the United States are supported, in part, by allowances from Church funds, i.e., by the voluntary alms of the faithful, sometimes called their "salary."

6. Diocesan priests in the United States are supported in part by Mass stipends and stole fees.

7. Diocesan priests in the United States are supported in part, at times, from non-ecclesiastical sources in exactly the same manner as any other citizen.

II

Conclusions of Law

1. The support of diocesan priests in the United States is of the same nature as the support of priests in the primitive Church.

2. Canon 1529 adopts as Canon Law the American Secular Law as to contracts and payments in the United States in respect to the *nature* of support of diocesan priests.

3. Support of diocesan priests in the United States must be, at Canon Law, either of the nature of "compensation" resulting from a contract or of the nature of a "gift."

4. The allowance from church funds, sometimes called "salary,"

received by diocesan priests in the United States is not of the same nature as "salary" received under a contract of employment or statutory enactment, but is identical in its nature with the *congrua* or *congrua sustentatio* received by the priests in the primitive Church, and therefore is of the nature of a gift.

5. There is no contract whatsoever, at law, between a diocesan priest and his bishop, under which a priest receives his support.

6. Support received by a diocesan priest in the United States from an ecclesiastical benefice, office, or subsidy, is of the legal nature of a gift.

7. Support received by a diocesan priest in the United States from Mass stipends and stole fees is of the legal nature of a gift.

8. Support received by a diocesan priest in the United States from other than the above mentioned ecclesiastical sources, received by him not as priest but as a citizen, is, because of its non-ecclesiastical source, received outside the scope of the jurisdiction of the Church, and depends exclusively on the laws of the United States for the determination of its nature; this nature is identical with the nature of similar support received by any other citizen.

9. Some legal effects in secular law of the nature of support of diocesan priests in the United States deal with the Income Tax, the Social Security Laws, and Workmen's Compensation. It is submitted that, because of its nature as a gift, support received by a diocesan priest from ecclesiastical sources is not subject to an Income Tax whether Federal, State, or Municipal, Social Security Tax, or to any Workmen's Compensation Acts.

APPENDIX

All The Reported Cases in American Courts of Record Involving Mass Stipends to January 1, 1949

ALABAMA

Festorazzi v. St. Joseph's Catholic Church......1893
104 Alabama 327.

CALIFORNIA

Estate of Anna Herzo......1902
2 Coffey's Probate 165.
Estate of Lennon......1907
152 California 327.
Rutherford v. Ott......1918
37 Cal. App. 47.
Estate of Hamilton......1919
181 California 758.
Estate of Margaret Ward......1932
125 Cal. App. 717.
Estate of Hurley......1935
Probate Court Los Angeles County, No. 156,254.
Estate of Corr......1941
Probate Court Los Angeles County, No. 199,619.
Estate of Dubbel......1941
Probate Court Los Angeles County, No. 210,016.
Estate of Colburn......1944
Probate Court Los Angeles County, No. 230,393.

DELAWARE

Delaware Trust Co. v. Fitzmaurice......1943
31 Atl. Rep. 2d. 383.
Satterfield v. Begley, et al......1945
43 Atl. Rep. 2d. 246.

DISTRICT OF COLUMBIA

Newton v. Carberry......1840
5 Cranch C.C. 626; 18 Federal Cases; Case No. 10,189.
Newton v. Carberry......1840
5 Cranch C.C. 632; 18 Federal Cases; Case No. 10,190.
Horn v. Foley......1898
13 App. Cas. Dist. of Col. 184.

Cunningham v. Dist. of Col. 1941
Bd. of Tax Appeals, D. of C.; Opinion No. 255.
Sedgwick v. Nat. Sav. & Trust Co. 1942
130 Fed. 2d. 440.

ILLINOIS

Kehoe v. Kehoe 1883
Circuit Ct. of Cook Co. In note to *Gilman v. McArdle,* 12 Abb. N.C. (N.Y.) 427.
Hoeffer v. Clogan 1898
171 Ill. 462.
Gilmore v. Lee 1908
237 Ill. 402.
Burke v. Burke 1913
259 Ill. 262.

INDIANA

Ackerman v. Fichter 1913
179 Ind. 392.
Cornet v. Guedelhoefer 1941
36 N.E. 2d. 933.

IOWA

Seda v. Huble 1888
75 Iowa 429.
Moran v. Moran 1897
104 Iowa 216.
Wilmes v. Tiernay 1919
187 Iowa 390.

KANSAS

Harrison v. Brophy 1898
59 Kan. 1.

KENTUCKY

Coleman v. O'Leary's Ex'r 1902
114 Ky. 388.
Obrecht v. Pujos 1925
206 Ky. 751.
Ramsey v. Mahoney's Ex'r 1944
297 Ky. 62.

MASSACHUSETTS

James Schouler, Petitioner 1883
134 Mass. 426.
Mahoney v. Nollman 1941
309 Mass. 522.

Minnesota

Shanahan v. Kelly............1903
88 Minn. 202.

Missouri

Schmucker's Estate v. Reel............1876
61 Mo. 592.
Minturn v. Conception Abbey............1933
227 Missouri Appeals 1179.
In re Flynn's Estate............1940
Flynn v. O'Reilly et al.
St. Louis Court of Appeals; 142 S.W. 2d. 1069.

New Hampshire

Webster v. Sughrow............1898
69 N. H. 380.

New Jersey

Kerrigan v. Tabb et al.............1898
39 Atlantic 701.
Kerrigan v. Conelly............1900
46 Atlantic 227.
Moran v. Kelley............1924
(95 N. J. Eq. 380); 96 N. J. Eq. 699.
Chelsea Nat. Bank v. Our Lady Star of the Sea Church............1929
147 Atlantic 470.
Gallagher v. Venturini............1938
124 N. J. Eq. 538.

New York

Hagenmeyer v. Hanselman............1883
12 Abbott's New Cases 432.
In re O'Hara's Will............1884
95 N.Y. 403.
Gilman v. McArdle............1885
99 N.Y. 451.
Holland v. Alcock............1888
108 N.Y. 312.
In re Schwartz's Will............1888
3 N.Y.S. 134.
O'Conner v. Gifford............1889
117 N.Y. 275.
In re Black's Estate............1889
5 N.Y.S. 452.
Ruppel v. Schlegel et al.............1889
7 N.Y.S. 936.

Vanderveer v. McKane..1890
11 N.Y.S. 808.
Estate of Julia Howard..1893
25 N.Y.S. 1111.
Will of Backes..1894
9 Misc. 504.
In re Zimmerman's Will..1898
22 Misc. 411.
Ellen Morris, Admx. v. Hughes..1904
45 Misc. 278.
Hoffman v. Union Dime Sav. Inst..1905
109 App. Div. 24.
Estate of Mary J. McAvoy..1906
112 App. Div. 377.
Johnston v. Hughes et al..1907
80 N.E. 373.
Morris v. Wucher..1907
(115 App. Div. 278) ; 188 N. Y. 568.
In re Didion's Estate..1907
54 Misc. 201.
In re O'Regan's Will..1909
62 Misc. 592.
Matter of Eppig..1909
63 Misc. 613.
Estate of Rywolt..1913
81 Misc. 103.
Petition of Catherine J. Welch..1918
105 Misc. 27.
Morris v. Edwards..1919
227 N. Y. 141.
In re Dwyer..1920
182 N.Y.S. 64.
In re Beck's Estate..1927
130 Misc. 765.
Matter of Brown..1929
135 Misc. 611.
Estate of Werrick..1930
135 Misc. 876.
Matter of Smallman..1931
138 Misc. 889.
Estate of Cunningham..1931
140 Misc. 91.
Matter of McArdle..1933
147 Misc. 876.

Estate of Abraham Stephen....................1934
150 Misc. 27.
Matter of Semenza....................1936
159 Misc. 487.
In re Korzeniewska's Estate....................1937
297 N.Y.S. 997.
In re Idem's Will....................1939
256 App. Div. 124.
Estate of Breckwoldt....................1941
176 Misc. 549.
In re De Molina's Estate....................1942
35 N.Y.S. 2d. 24.
In re Hofmeister's Estate....................1944
48 N.Y.S. 2d. 351.

OHIO Date uncertain—but

Fugmann et al. v. Chrystomus Theobald....................after 1895
12 C.D. 720
In re Estate of Henry Brinkman....................1897
38 Weekly Law Bulletin 304.
In re Estate of Emma Muennich....................1920
Probate Court Cuyahoga County.
Dempsey, Ex'x v. Christ the King Church....................
Probate Court Cuyahoga County.
Tax Commissioner v. Gerdeman....................(unreported)
Court of Appeals of Putnam County, No. 200.
In re Estate of Reilly....................1941
138 Ohio State 145.
Mosbacher v. Alter....................1946
66 N.E. 2d. 774.

PENNSYLVANIA

Ex'rs of Browers v. Fromm....................1798
Addison's Rep. 361.
McGirr v. Aaron....................1829
1 Pen. & Watts 49.
Ann Dougherty's Estate....................1878
12 Phila. 70.
Rhymer's Appeal....................1880
93 Pa. St. 142.
Appeal of Seibert....................1886
18 W.N.C. 276.
Kelly's Estate....................1900
9 Penn. Dist. 387.

O'Donnell's Estate............1904
209 Pa. 63.
Estate of Moran............1906
24 Lancaster L.R. 70.
Nead's Estate............1914
55 Penn. Sup'r 573.
Farrell's Estate............1921
1 Penn. D. & Co. 128.
Loughran's Estate............1922
2 Pa. D. & Co. 223.
Estate of Meyer............1928
31 Dauphin Co. 304.
Jenning's Estate............1934
20 Pa. D. & Co. 506.
Thornton v. Koch et al............1935
176 Atl. 3.
Ross v. Philadelphia et al............1942
25 Atlantic 2d. 834.

RHODE ISLAND

Sherman v. Baker............1898
20 R. I. 446.
Slattery v. Ward............1923
45 R. I. 54.

WISCONSIN

McHugh v. McCole............1897
97 Wisc. 166.
Will of Kavanaugh............1910
143 Wisc. 90.

UNITED STATES

Gonzales v. Roman Catholic Archbishop............1929
280 U. S. 1.

BIBLIOGRAPHY

SOURCES

Acta Apostolicae Sedis, Commentarium Officiale, Romae, 1909—

Acta et Decreta Concilii Plenarii Baltimorensis Tertii, A.D. 1884, Baltimorae; Typis Joannis Murphy Sociorum, 1886.

Acta et Decreta Sacrorum Conciliorum Recentiorum, Collectio Lacensis, 7 vols., Friburgi Brisgoviae: Herder, 1870-1892.

Acta et Decreta Synodi Dioecesanae Toletanae Primae, 1941, Toleti, Cancelleria Curiae Dioecesanae, 1941.

Bruns, Hermann T., *Canones Apostolorum et Conciliorum Saeculorum IV, V, VI, VII,* 2 vols., Berolini, 1839.

Code of Federal Regulations of the United States of America, The, 15 vols. in 17 & index, with Cumulative Supplements, Washington, D.C., United States Government Printing Office, 1939—

Codex Iuris Canonici Pii X Pontificis Maximi iussu digestus Benedicti Papae XV auctoritate promulgatus, Romae: Typis Polyglottis Vaticanis, 1917.

Codicis Iuris Canonici Fontes, cura Emi Petri Card. Gasparri editi, 9 vols., Romae (postea Civitate Vaticana), Typis Polyglottis Vaticanis, 1923-1939. (Vols. VII-IX ed. cura et studio Emi Iustiniani Card. Seredi.)

Collectanea S. Congregationis de Propaganda Fide, 2 vols., Romae: Typographia Polyglotta S. C. de Propaganda Fide, 1907. (Vol. I, nn. 1-1299; Vol. II, nn. 1300-2317.)

Corpus Juris, Being a Complete and Systematic Statement of the Whole Body of the Law, edited by William Mack, LL.D., and Donald J. Kiser, LL. D., 71 vols., New York: The American Law Book Co., 1914-1935.

Corpus Iuris Canonici, editio Lipsiensis secunda, post Aemilii Richteri curas, instruxit Aemilius Friedberg, 2 vols., Lipsiae, 1879-1881.

Du Cange, Charles du Fresne, *Glossarium ad Scriptores Mediae et Infimae Latinitatis,* 10 vols., ed. L. Favre, Niort, 1883-1887.

Hearings before the Committee on Finance, United States Senate, Seventy-Sixth Congress, First Session, on HR 6635, revised print, Washington: United States Government Printing Office, 1939.

Hearings Relative to the Social Security Act Amendments of 1939 before the Committee on Ways and Means, House of Representatives, Seventy-Sixth Congress, First Session, revised print, Washington: United States Government Printing Office, 1939.

Jaffé, Phillipus, *Regesta Pontificum Romanorum ab condita Ecclesia ad annum post Christum natum MCXCVIII*, 2 ed., correctam et auctam auspiciis Gulielmi Wattenbach curaverunt S. Löwenfeld, F. Kaltenbrunner, P. Ewald, 2 tomes in 1 vol., Lipsiae, 1885-1888.

Mansi, Joannes, *Sacrorum Conciliorum Nova et Amplissima Collectio*, 53 vols. in 60, Parisiis, 1901-1927.

Monumenta Germaniae Historica, Legum Sectio III, Concilia, Tomus II, Pars I, *Concilia Aevi Karolini I.*, ed. A. Werminghoff, Hannoverae et Lipsiae, Bibliopolii Hahman, 1906.

New Testament, The, Translated from the Latin Vulgate under the Patronage of the Episcopal Committee of the Confraternity of Christian Doctrine, Patterson, New Jersey: St. Anthony Guild Press, 1941.

Restatement of the Law of Agency, 2 vols., St. Paul: American Law Institute Publishers, 1933.

Restatement of the Law of Conflict of Laws, St. Paul: American Law Institute Publishers, 1934.

Restatement of the Law of Contracts, 2 vols., St. Paul: American Law Institute Publishers, 1932.

Restatement of the Law of Trusts, 2 vols., St. Paul: American Law Institute Publishers, 1935.

S. Romanae Rotae Decisiones seu Sententiae quae . . . prodierunt anno 1909— , Romae: Typis Polyglottis Vaticanis, 1912—

Thiel, A., *Epistolae Romanorum Pontificum genuinae a S. Hilario (461-468) usque ad S. Hormisdam (514-523)*, Brunsbergae, 1868.

United States Code, 1946 ed., 50 Titles, Washington: United States Government Printing Office, 1947.

United States Government, Treasury Department, Bureau of Internal Revenue, *Official Instructions, How To Prepare Your U.S. Income Tax Return on Form 1040 for 1948*, Washington: U. S. Government Printing Office, 1948.

AUTHORS

Allen, G. F., *De Existentia Beneficiorum Paroecialium ante et post Codicem in Statibus Foederatis Americae*, Romae: Anonima Libraria Cattolica Italiana, 1938.

Aquinas, St. Thomas, *Summa Theologica*, ed. Marietti, 6 vols., Taurino Romae: Marietti, 1937.

Augustine, C., *The Canonical and Civil Status of Catholic Parishes in the United States*, St. Louis: Herder Book Co., 1926.

Barrett, J., *A Comparative Study of the Third Plenary Council of Baltimore and the Code*, The Catholic University of America Canon Law Studies, n. 83, Washington: The Catholic University of America, 1932.

Blackstone, W., *Commentaries on the Law of England,* 12 ed., 4 vols., Dublin, 1775.

Berutti, C., *Institutiones Iuris Canonici,* 6 vols. in 7 (Vol. II, Pars II,et Vol. V nondum edita), Taurini: Marietti, 1936—

Blat, A., *Commentarium Textus Codicis Iuris Canonici,* 6 vols., Romae: Libreria del Collegio "Angelico," 1919-1927.

Bouscaren, T. Lincoln, *The Canon Law Digest,* 2 vols., Milwaukee: The Bruce Publishing Co., 1934-1943.

Brunini, J., *The Clerical Obligations of Canons 139 and 142,* The Catholic University of America Canon Law Studies, n. 103, Washington, D. C.: The Catholic University of America, 1937.

Brys, J., *Juris Canonici Compendium,* Brugis: Desclée de Brouwer et Sii, 1947.

Cance, A., *Le Code de Droit Canonique,* 2 ed., 3 vols., Paris: Gabalda et Fils, 1929.

Cappello, F., *Tractatus Canonico-moralis de Sacramentis,* 4 ed., 3 vols. in 6, Taurinorum Augustae: Marietti, 1939-1945.

———, *Summa Iuris Canonici,* 2 ed., 3 vols., Romae: apud Aedes Universitatis Gregorianae, 1932-1940.

Cleary, J., *The Canonical Limitations on the Alienation of Church Property,* The Catholic University of America Canon Law Studies, n. 100, Washington, D. C.: The Catholic University of America, 1936.

Cocchi, G., *Commentarium in Codicem Iuris Canonici,* 5 vols. in 8, 4 ed., Taurinorum Augustae: Marietti, 1931-1942.

Comyns, J., *Papal and Episcopal Administration of Church Property,* The Catholic University of America Canon Law Studies, n. 147, Washington, D. C.: The Catholic University of America Press, 1942.

Coronata, Matthaeus Conte a, *Institutiones Iuris Canonici,* 2 ed., 5 vols., Taurini: Marietti, 1939-1947.

———, *Institutiones Iuris Canonici ad usum utriusque cleri et scholarum: De Sacramentis Tractatus Canonicus,* 3 vols., Taurini: Marietti, 1943-1946.

D'Achery, L., *Spicilegium sive collectio veterum aliquot scriptorum,* Parisiis, 1723.

D'Angelo, S., *Le Tasse e le Pensioni nel Codice di diritto Canonico,* 2 ed., cor. ed. ampl., Torino: L. I. C. E., 1927.

De Meester, A., *Juris Canonici et Juris Canonico-Civilis Compendium* ed. nova. 3 vols. in 4, Brugis: Desclée de Brouwer et Si., 1921-1928.

De Rozière, E., *Liber Diurnus,* Paris, 1869.

Ferry, W., *Stole Fees,* The Catholic University of America Canon Law Studies, n. 59, Washington, D. C.: The Catholic University of America, 1930.

Findlay, S., *Canonical Norms Governing the Deposition and Degradation of Clerics,* The Catholic University of America Canon Law Studies, n. 130, Washington, D. C.: The Catholic University of America Press, 1941.

Funk, F. X., *Patres Apostolici,* 2 vols., Tübingen, H. Laupp, 1901.

Gasparri, P., *Schema Codicis Iuris Canonici,* Romae: Typis Polyglottis Vaticanis, 1913.

———, *Tractatus Canonicus de Sanctissima Eucharistia,* 2 vols., Paris: Delhomme et Briguet, 1897.

Gass, S., *Ecclesiastical Pensions,* The Catholic University of America Canon Law Studies, n. 157, Washington, D. C.: The Catholic University of America Press, 1942.

Guilday, P., *A History of the Councils of Baltimore, 1791-1884,* New York: The Macmillan Company, 1932.

———, (Editor), *National Pastorals of the American Hierarchy,* Washington, D. C.: N.C.W.C., 1923.

Heston, E., *The Alienation of Church Property in the United States,* The Catholic University of America Canon Law Studies, n. 132, Washington, D. C.: The Catholic University of America Press, 1941.

Hughes, T., *History of the Society of Jesus in North America, Colonial and Federal,* 4 vols., Text: 2 vols., Documents: 2 vols., New York: Longmans Green & Co., 1907-1917.

Keller, C., *Mass Stipends,* The Catholic University of America Canon Law Studies, n. 27, Washington, D. C.: The Catholic University of America, 1925.

Kremer, M., *Church Support in the United States,* The Catholic University of America Canon Law Studies, n. 61, Washington, D. C.: The Catholic University of America, 1930.

Landon, E. H., *A Manual of Councils of the Holy Catholic Church,* new and rev. ed., 2 vols., Edinburgh: John Grant, reprint in 1909.

Manning, J., *The Free Conferral of Offices,* The Catholic University of America Canon Law Studies, n. 219, Washington, D. C.: The Catholic University of America Press, 1945.

Many, S., *Praelectiones de Missa,* Paris: Letouzey et Ane, 1903.

McClunn, J., *Administrative Recourse,* The Catholic University of America Canon Law Studies, n. 240, Washington, D. C.: The Catholic University of America Press, 1946.

McDevitt, G., *The Renunciation of an Ecclesiastical Office,* The Catholic University of America Canon Law Studies, n. 218, Washington, D. C.: The Catholic University of America Press, 1946.

Meier, C., *Penal Administrative Procedure Against Negligent Pastors,* The Catholic University of America Canon Law Studies, n. 140, Washington, D. C.: The Catholic University of America Press, 1941.

Merkelbach, B., *Summa Theologiae Moralis ad Mentem D. Thomae et ad Normam Juris Novi,* 3 ed., 3 vols., Parisiis: Typis Desclée de Brouwer et Soc.. 1938-1939.

Mertens, J., *The Law of Federal Income Taxation,* 12 vols., Chicago: Callaghan and Co., 1942.

Migne, J. P., *Patrologiae Cursus Completus, Series Latina,* 221 vols., Parisiis, 1844-1864.

Miller, N., *Founded Masses According to the Code of Canon Law,* The Catholic University of America Canon Law Studies, n. 34, Washington, D. C.: The Catholic University of America, 1926.

Montgomery, R., *Montgomery's Federal Taxes,* 1947-1948 edition, New York: The Ronald Press Co., 1948.

Mourret, F.-Thompson, N., *History of the Catholic Church,* 6 vols., St. Louis: B. Herder Co., 1930-1945.

Murphy, F., *Legislative Powers of the Provincial Council,* The Catholic University of America Canon Law Studies, n. 257, Washington, D. C.: The Catholic University of America Press, 1947.

Noldin, H.-Schmidt, A., *Summa Theologiae Moralis,* 27 ed., 3 vols., Oeniponte/Lipsiae: Sumptibus et Typis Feliciani Rauch, 1940-1941.

Pistocchi, M., *De Re Beneficiali iuxta Canones Codicis Iuris Canonici,* Taurini: Marietti, 1928.

Regatillo, E., *Institutiones Iuris Canonici,* 2 vols., Santander: Sal Terrae, 1941-1942.

———, *Ius Sacramentarium,* 2 vols., Santander: Sal Terrae, 1945-1946.

Richardson, J., *The Just Title in Canon 730 for giving something temporal on the occasion of the Sacred Ministry,* Romae: Institutum Pontificium Internationale Angelicum, 1936.

Roberti, F., *Respectus Sociales in Codice Iuris Canonici,* Romae: Apollinaris, 1937.

Ryan, G., *Principles of Episcopal Jurisdiction,* The Catholic University of America Canon Law Studies, n. 120, Washington, D. C.: The Catholic University of America Press, 1939.

Ryder, R., *Simony,* The Catholic University of America Canon Law Studies, n. 65, Washington, D. C.: The Catholic University of America, 1931.

Santi, F., *Praelectiones Juris Canonici,* 2 vols., Ratisbon, New York and Cincinnati: Pustet, 1886.

Schmalzgrueber, F., *Jus Ecclesiasticum Universum,* 5 vols. in 12, Romae, 1843-1845.

Scott, Austin W., *The Law of Trusts,* 4 vols., Boston: Little Brown and Company, 1939.

Sipos, S., *Enchiridion Iuris Canonici,* 3 ed., Pécs: Haladás R.T., 1936.

Thomassinus, L., *Vetus et Nova Ecclesiae Disciplina,* Magontiaci, 1787.

Toso, A., *Ad Codicem Juris Canonici . . . Commentaria Minora,* 5 vols. in 2, Taurini: Marietti, 1918-1927.

Vermeersch, A., *Theologia Moralis,* 3 ed., 4 vols., Romae: Pontificia Università Gregoriana, Reimpressio, 1945.

Vermeersch, A.-Creusen, J., *Epitome Iuris Canonici,* 3 vols., Vols. I and II, 2 ed., 1923-1925; Vol. III, 6 ed., 1946 Mechliniae-Romae: Dessain.

Vromant, G., *De Bonis Ecclesiae Temporalibus,* Museum Lessianum, Section Théologique, n. 19, Louvain: Museum Lessianum, 1927.

Wernz, F., *Ius Decretalium,* 6 vols., Romae et Prati, 1898-1905.

Wernz, F.-Vidal, P., *Ius Canonicum ad Codicis Normam Exactum,* 7 vols. in 8, Romae: apud Aedes Universitatis Gregorianae, 1923-1938.

Williston, S., *The Law of Contracts, A Treatise on,* 8 vols., New York: Baker, Voorhis & Co., 1936.

Zollmann, C., *American Church Law,* St. Paul: West Publishing Co., 1933.

ARTICLES

Allen, W., "The Parish-Benefice Revenue,"—*The Jurist,* VIII (1948), 323-332.

Anonymous, "Fees and Stipends,"—*The Jurist,* I (1941), 335-342.

Hannan, J., "The Cleric's Last Will,"—*The Jurist,* VIII (1948), 41-61.

Horovitz, "Current Trends in Basic Principles of Workmen's Compensation,"—*The Law Society Journal,* XII (1947), 465-477.

Lennon, M., "The Priest and the Victory Tax,"—*The Jurist,* III (1943), 441-453.

O'Brien, D. E., Book Review of "The First Freedom,"—*Notre Dame Lawyer,* XXIV (1948) 134-140.

O'Brien, K. R., "The Parish Priest and the Federal Income Tax under the Revenue Act of 1942,"—*The Jurist,* III (1943), 129-145.

———, "The Priest and the Victory Tax—Replication,"—*The Jurist,* III (1943), 452-456.

———, "Foundations for Masses Should Never Create Trusts,"—*The Jurist,* IV (1944), 284-317.

O'Brien, K. R.—O'Brien, D. E., "How New York Restricts Gifts for Masses,"—*Fordham Law Review,* XIII (1944), 175-192.

———, "Freedom of Religion in Restatement of Inter-Church-and-State Common Law,"—*The Jurist,* VI (1946), 503-523.

Pound, R., "A Comparison of the Ideals of Law,"—*Harvard Law Review,* XLVII (1933), 1-17.

Roelker, E., "The Right to Revenue During Non-Residence,"—*The Jurist,* I (1941), 74-76.

White, Robert, Book Review of "American Church Law,"—*Harvard Law Review,* XLVII (1933), 377-378.

PERIODICALS

Fordham Law Review, New York, 1932-

Harvard Law Review, Cambridge, Massachusetts, 1887-

Law Society Journal, Boston, Massachusetts, 1935-

The Jurist, Washington, D. C., 1941-

The New York Times, New York, 1896-

Notre Dame Lawyer, South Bend, Indiana, 1924-

SPECIAL INDEX

Secular Cases Cited. (References are to pages).

GENERAL INDEX

NOTE: This index is to notes as well as to text. Indentation is used to avoid repetition of wording. References are to pages.

S

W

BIOGRAPHICAL NOTE

Kenneth Robert O'Brien was born on February 20, 1915, in Beverly, Massachusetts. He received the degree of Bachelor of Arts from St. Patrick's Seminary, Menlo Park, California, in 1936. He was ordained to the priesthood in 1940. In 1946 he was assigned to studies at The Catholic University of America where he received the degree of Bachelor in Canon Law in June, 1947, and the degree of Licentiate in Canon Law in June, 1948.

CANON LAW STUDIES*

1. FRERIKS, REV. CELESTINE A., C.PP.S., J.C.D., Religious Congregations in Their External Relations, 121 pp., 1916.
2. GALLIHER, REV. DANIEL M., O.P., J.C.D., Canonical Elections, 117 pp., 1917.
3. BORKOWSKI, REV. AURELIUS L., O.F.M., J.C.D., De Confraternitatibus Ecclesiasticis, 136 pp., 1918.
4. CASTILLO, REV. CAYO, J.C.D., Disertacion Historico-Canonica sobre la Potestad del Cabildo en Sede Vacante o Impedida del Vicario Capitular, 99 pp., 1919 (1918).
5. KUBELBECK, REV. WILLIAM J., S.T.B., J.C.D., The Sacred Penitentiaria and Its Relation to Faculties of Ordinaries and Priests, 129 pp., 1918.
6. PETROVITS, REV. JOSEPH J. C., S.T.D., J.C.D., The New Church Law on Matrimony, X-461 pp., 1919.
7. HICKEY, REV. JOHN J., S.T.B., J.C.D., Irregularities and Simple Impediments in the New Code of Canon Law, 100 pp., 1920.
8. KLEKOTKA, REV. PETER J., S.T.B., J.C.D., Diocesan Consultors, 179 pp., 1920.
9. WANENMACHER, REV. FRANCIS, J.C.D., The Evidence in Ecclesiastical Procedure Affecting the Marriage Bond, 1920 (Printed 1935).
10. GOLDEN, REV. HENRY FRANCIS, J.C.D., Parochial Benefices in the New Code, IV-119 pp., 1921 (Printed 1925).
11. KOUDELKA, REV. CHARLES J., J.C.D., Pastors, Their Rights and Duties According to the New Code of Canon Law, 211 pp., 1921.
12. MELO, REV. ANTONIUS, O.F.M., J.C.D., De Exemptione Regularium, X-188 pp., 1921.
13. SCHAAF, REV. VALENTINE THEODORE, O.F.M., S.T.B., J.C.D., The Cloister, X-180 pp., 1921.
14. BURKE, REV. THOMAS JOSEPH, S.T.D., J.C.D., Competence in Ecclesiastical Tribunals, IV-117 pp., 1922.
15. LEECH, REV. GEORGE LEO, J.C.D., A Comparative Study of the Constitution "Apostolicae Sedis" and the "Codex Juris Canonici," 179 pp., 1922.
16. MOTRY, REV. HUBERT LOUIS, S.T.D., J.C.D., Diocesan Faculties According to the Code of Canon Law, II-167 pp., 1922.
17. MURPHY, REV. GEORGE LAWRENCE, J.C.D., Delinquencies and Penalties in the Administration and the Reception of the Sacraments, IV-121 pp., 1923.

* From nn. 1-100 inclusive only n. 25 is still obtainable. From n. 101 onward all numbers are available except the following: 101-114, 116, 118, 120, 122, 123 and 162.

18. O'REILLY, REV. JOHN ANTHONY, S.T.B., J.C.D., Ecclesiastical Sepulture in the New Code of Canon Law, II-129 pp., 1923.
19. MICHALICKA, REV. WENCESLAS CYRILL, O.S.B., J.C.D., Judicial Procedure in Dismissal of Clerical Exempt Religious, 107 pp., 1923.
20. DARGIN, REV. EDWARD VINCENT, S.T.B., J.C.D., Reserved Cases According to the Code of Canon Law, IV-103 pp., 1924.
21. GODFREY, REV. JOHN A., S.T.B., J.C.D., The Right of Patronage According to the Code of Canon Law, 153 pp., 1924.
22. HAGEDORN, REV. FRANCIS EDWARD, J.C.D., General Legislation on Indulgences, II-154 pp., 1924.
23. KING, REV. JAMES IGNATIUS, J.C.D., The Administration of the Sacraments to Dying Non-Catholics, V-141 pp., 1924.
24. WINSLOW, REV. FRANCIS JOSEPH, M.M., J.C.D., Vicars and Prefects Apostolic, IV-149 pp., 1924.
25. CORREA, REV. JOSE SERVELION, S.T.L., J.C.D., La Potestad Legislativa de la Iglesia Catolica, IV-127 pp., 1925.
26. DUGAN, REV. HENRY FRANCIS, A.M., J.C.D., The Judiciary Department of the Diocesan Curia, 87 pp., 1925.
27. KELLER, REV. CHARLES FREDERICK, S.T.B., J.C.D., Mass Stipends, 167 pp., 1925.
28. PASCHANG, REV. JOHN LINUS, J.C.D., The Sacramentals According to the Code of Canon Law, 129 pp., 1925.
29. PIONTEK, REV. CYRILLUS, O.F.M., S.T.B., J.C.D., De Indulto Exclaustrationis necnon Saecularizationis, XIII-289 pp., 1925.
30. KEARNEY, REV. RICHARD JOSEPH, S.T.B., J.C.D., Sponsors at Baptism According to the Code of Canon Law, IV-127 pp., 1925.
31. BARTLETT, REV. CHESTER JOSEPH, A.M., LL.B., J.C.D., The Tenure of Parochial Property in the United States of America, V-108 pp., 1926.
32. KILKER, REV. ADRIAN JEROME, J.C.D., Extreme Unction, V-425 pp., 1926.
33. MCCORMICK, REV. ROBERT EMMETT, J.C.D., Confessors of Religious, VIII-266 pp., 1926.
34. MILLER, REV. NEWTON THOMAS, J.C.D., Founded Masses According to the Code of Canon Law, VII-93 pp., 1926.
35. ROELKER, REV. EDWARD G., S.T.D., J.C.D., Principles of Privilege According to the Code of Canon Law, XI-166 pp., 1926.
36. BAKALARCZYK, REV. RICHARDUS, M.I.C., J.U.D., De Novitiatu, VII-208 pp., 1927.
37. PIZZUTI, REV. LAWRENCE, O.F.M., J.U.L., De Parochis Religiosis, 1927. (Not Printed.)
38. BLILEY, REV. NICHOLAS MARTIN, O.S.B., J.C.D., Altars According to the Code of Canon Law, XIX-132 pp., 1927.
39. BROWN, MR. BRENDAN FRANCIS, A.B., LL.M., J.U.D., The Canonical Juristic Personality with Special Reference to its Status in the United States of America, V-212 pp., 1927.

40. Cavanaugh, Rev. William Thomas, C.P., J.U.D., The Reservation of the Blessed Sacrament, VIII-101 pp., 1927.
41. Doheny, Rev. William J., C.S.C., A.B., J.U.D., Church Property: Modes of Acquisition, X-118 pp., 1927.
42. Feldhaus, Rev. Aloysius H., C.PP.S., J.C.D., Oratories, IX-141 pp., 1927.
43. Kelly, Rev. James Patrick, A.B., J.C.D., The Jurisdiction of the Simple Confessor, X-208 pp., 1927.
44. Neuberger, Rev. Nicholas J., J.C.D., Canon 6 or the Relation of the Codex Juris Canonici to the Preceding Legislation, V-95 pp., 1927.
45. O'Keefe, Rev. Gerald Michael, J.C.D., Matrimonial Dispensations, Powers of Bishops, Priests, and Confessors, VIII-232 pp., 1927.
46. Quigley, Rev. Joseph A. M., A.B., J.C.D., Condemned Societies, 139 pp., 1927.
47. Zaplotnik, Rev. Johannes Leo, J.C.D., De Vicariis Foraneis, X-142 pp., 1927.
48. Duskie, Rev. John Aloysius, A.B., J.C.D., The Canonical Status of the Orientals in the United States, VIII-196 pp., 1928.
49. Hyland, Rev. Francis Edward, J.C.D., Excommunication, Its Nature, Historical Development and Effects, VIII-181 pp., 1928.
50. Reinmann, Rev. Gerald Joseph, O.M.C., J.C.D., The Third Order Secular of Saint Francis, 201 pp., 1928.
51. Schenk, Rev. Francis J., J.C.D., The Matrimonial Impediments of Mixed Religion and Disparity of Cult, XVI-318 pp., 1929.
52. Coady, Rev. John Joseph, S.T.D., J.U.D., A.M., The Appointment of Pastors, VIII-150 pp., 1929.
53. Kay, Rev. Thomas Henry, J.C.D., Competence in Matrimonial Procedure, VIII-164 pp., 1929.
54. Turner, Rev. Sidney Joseph, C.P., J.U.D., The Vow of Poverty, XLIX-217 pp., 1929.
55. Kearney, Rev. Raymond A., A.B., S.T.D., J.C.D., The Principles of Delegation, VII-149 pp., 1929.
56. Conran, Rev. Edward James, A.B., J.C.D., The Interdict, V-163 pp., 1930.
57. O'Neill, Rev. William H., J.C.D., Papal Rescripts of Favor, VII-218 pp., 1930.
58. Bastnagel, Rev. Clement Vincent, J.U.D., The Appointment of Parochial Adjutants and Assistants, XV-257 pp., 1930.
59. Ferry, Rev. William A., A.B., J.C.D., Stole Fees, V-136 pp., 1930.
60. Costello, Rev. John Michael, A.B., J.C.D., Domicile and Quasi-Domicile, VII-201 pp., 1930.
61. Kremer, Rev. Michael Nicholas, A.B., S.T.B., J.C.D., Church Support in the United States, VI-136 pp., 1930.
62. Angulo, Rev. Luis, C.M., J.C.D., Legislation de la Iglesia sobre la intencion en la application de la Santa Misa, VII-104 pp., 1931.

63. Frey, Rev. Wolfgang Norbert, O.S.B., A.B., J.C.D., The Act of Religious Profession, VIII-174 pp., 1931.
64. Roberts, Rev. James Brendan, A.B., J.C.D., The Banns of Marriage, XIV-140 pp., 1931.
65. Ryder, Rev. Raymond Aloysius, A.B., J.C.D., Simony, IX-151 pp., 1931.
66. Campagna, Rev. Angelo, Ph.D., J.U.D., Il Vicario Generale del Vescovo, VII-205 pp., 1931.
67. Cox, Rev. Joseph Godfrey, A.B., J.C.D., The Administration of Seminaries, VI-124 pp., 1931.
68. Gregory, Rev. Donald J., J.U.D., The Pauline Privilege, XV-165 pp., 1931.
69. Donohue, Rev. John F., J.C.D., The Impediment of Crime, VII-110 pp., 1931.
70. Dooley, Rev. Eugene A., O.M.I., J.C.D., Church Law on Sacred Relics, IX-143 pp., 1931.
71. Orth, Rev. Clement Raymond, O.M.C., J.C.D., The Approbation of Religious Institutes, 171 pp., 1931.
72. Pernicone, Rev. Joseph M., A.B., J.C.D., The Ecclesiastical Prohibition of Books, XII-267 pp., 1932.
73. Clinton, Rev. Connell, A.B., J.C.D., The Paschal Precept, IX-108 pp., 1932.
74. Donnelly, Rev. Francis B., A.M., S.T.L., J.C.D., The Diocesan Synod, VIII-125 pp., 1932.
75. Torrente, Rev. Camilo, C.M.F., J.C.D., Las Procesiones Sagradas, V-145 pp., 1932.
76. Murphy, Rev. Edwin J., C.PP.S., J.C.D., Suspension Ex Informata Conscientia, XI-122 pp., 1932.
77. MacKenzie, Rev. Eric F., A.M., S.T.L., J.C.D., The Delict of Heresy in its Commission, Penalization, Absolution, VII-124 pp., 1932.
78. Lyons, Rev. Avitus E., S.T.B., J.C.D., The Collegiate Tribunal of First Instance, XI-147, pp., 1932.
79. Connolly, Rev. Thomas A., J.C.D., Appeals, XI-195 pp., 1932.
80. Sangmeister, Rev. Joseph V., A.B., J.C.D., Force and Fear as Precluding Matrimonial Consent, V-211 pp., 1932.
81. Jaeger, Rev. Leo A., A.B., J.C.D., The Administration of Vacant and Quasi-Vacant Epispocal Sees in the United States, IX-229 pp., 1932.
82. Rimlinger, Rev. Herbert T., J.C.D., Error Invalidating Matrimonial Consent, VII-79 pp., 1932.
83. Barrett, Rev. John D. M., S.S., J.C.D., A Comparative Study of the Third Plenary Council of Baltimore and the Code, IX-221 pp., 1932.
84. Carberry, Rev. John J., Ph.D., S.T.D., J.C.D., The Juridical Form of Marriage, X-177 pp., 1934.
85. Dolan, Rev. John L., A.B., J.C.D., The Defensor Vinculi, XII-157 pp., 1934.

86. Hannan, Rev. Jerome D., A.M., S.T.D., LL.B., J.C.D., The Canon Law of Wills, IX-517 pp., 1934.
87. Lemieux, Rev. Delise A., A.M., J.C.D., The Sentence in Ecclesiastical Procedure, IX-131 pp., 1934.
88. O'Rourke, Rev. James J., A.B., J.C.D., Parish Registers, VII-109 pp., 1934.
89. Timlin, Rev. Bartholomew, O.F.M., A.M., J.C.D., Conditional Matrimonial Consent, X-381 pp., 1934.
90. Wahl, Rev. Francis X., A.B., J.C.D., The Matrimonial Impediments of Consanguinity and Affinity, VI-125 pp., 1934.
91. White, Rev. Robert J., A.B., LL.B., S.T.B., J.C.D., Canonical Ante-Nuptial Promises and the Civil Law, VI-152 pp., 1934.
92. Herrera, Rev. Antonio Parra, O.C.D., J.C.D., Legislacion Ecclesiastica sobra el Ayuno y la Abstinencia, XI-191 pp., 1935.
93. Kennedy, Rev. Edwin J., J.C.D., The Special Matrimonial Process in Cases of Evident Nullity, X-165 pp., 1935.
94. Manning, Rev. John J., A.B., J.C.D., Presumption of Law in Matrimonial Procedure, XI-111 pp., 1935.
95. Moeder, Rev. John M., J.C.D., The Proper Bishop for Ordination and Dismissorial Letters, VII-135 pp., 1935.
96. O'Mara, Rev. William A., A.B., J.C.D., Canonical Causes for Matrimonial Dispensations, IX-155 pp., 1935.
97. Reilly, Rev. Peter, J.C.D., Residence of Pastors, IX-81 pp., 1935.
98. Smith, Rev. Mariner T., O.P., S.T.Lr., J.C.D., The Penal Law for Religious, VII-169 pp., 1935.
99. Whalen, Rev. Donald W., A.M., J.C.D., The Value of Testimonial Evidence in Matrimonial Procedure, XIII-297 pp., 1935.
100. Cleary, Rev. Joseph F., J.C.D., Canonical Limitations on the Alienation of Church Property, VIII-141 pp., 1936.
101. Glynn, Rev. John C., J.C.D., The Promoter of Justice, XX-337 pp., 1936.
102. Brennan, Rev. James H., S.S., M.A., S.T.B., J.C.D., The Simple Convalidation of Marriage, VI-135 pp. 1937.
103. Brunini, Rev. Joseph Bernard, J.C.D., The Clerical Obligations of Canons 139 and 142, X-121 pp., 1937.
104. Connor, Rev. Maurice, A.B., J.C.D., The Administrative Removal of Pastors, VIII-159 pp., 1937.
105. Guilfoyle, Rev. Merlin Joseph, J.C.D., Custom, XI-144, pp., 1937.
106. Hughes, Rev. James Austin, A.B., A.M., J.C.D., Witnesses in Criminal Trials of Clerics, IX-140 pp., 1937.
107. Jansen, Rev. Raymond J., A.B., S.T.L., J.C.D., Canonical Provisions for Catechetical Instruction, VII-153 pp., 1937.
108. Kealy, Rev. John James, A.B., J.C.D., The Introductory Libellus in Church Court Procedure, XI-121 pp., 1937.

109. McManus, Rev. James Edward, C.SS.R., J.C.D., The Administration of Temporal Goods in Religious Institutes, XVI-196 pp., 1937.
110. Moriarty, Rev. Eugene James, J.C.D., Oaths in Ecclesiastical Courts, X-115 pp., 1937.
111. Rainer, Rev. Eligius George, C.SS.R., J.C.D., Suspension of Clerics, XVII-249 pp., 1937.
112. Reilly, Rev. Thomas F., C.SS.R., J.C.D., Visitation of Religious, VI-195 pp., 1938.
113. Moriarty, Rev. Francis E., C.SS.R., J.C.D., The Extraordinary Absolution from Censures, XV-334 pp., 1938.
114. Connolly, Rev. Nicholas P., J.C.D., The Canonical Erection of Parishes, X-132 pp., 1938.
115. Donovan, Rev. James Joseph, J.C.D., The Pastor's Obligation in Prenuptial Investigation, XII-322 pp., 1938.
116. Harrigan, Rev. Robert J., M.A., S.T.B., J.C.D., The Radical Sanation of Invalid Marriages, VIII-208 pp., 1938.
117. Boffa, Rev. Conrad Humbert, J.C.D., Canonical Provisions for Catholic Schools, VII-211 pp., 1939.
118. Parsons, Rev. Anscar John, O.M.Cap., J.C.D., Canonical Elections, XII-236 pp., 1939.
119. Reilly, Rev. Edward Michael, A.B., J.C.D., The General Norms of Dispensation, XII-156 pp., 1939.
120. Ryan, Rev. Gerald Aloysius, A.B., J.C.D., Principles of Episcopal Jurisdiction, XII-172 pp., 1939.
121. Burton, Rev. Francis James, C.S.C., A.B., J.C.D., A Commentary on Canon 1125, X-222 pp., 1940.
122. Miaskiewicz, Rev. Francis Sigismund, J.C.D., Supplied Jurisdiction According to Canon 209, XII-340 pp., 1940.
123. Rice, Rev. Patrick William, A.B., J.C.D., Proof of Death in Prenuptial Investigation, VIII-156 pp., 1940.
124. Anglin, Rev. Thomas Francis, M.S., J.C.D., The Eucharistic Fast, VIII-183 pp., 1941.
125. Coleman, Rev. John Jerome, J.C.D., The Minister of Confirmation, VI-153 pp., 1941.
126. Downs, Rev. John Emmanuel, A.B., J.C.D., The Concept of Clerical Immunity, XI-163 pp., 1941.
127. Esswein, Rev. Anthony Albert, J.C.D., Extrajudicial Penal Powers of Ecclesiastical Superiors, X-144 pp., 1941.
128. Farrell, Rev. Benjamin Francis, M.A., S.T.L., J.C.D., The Rights and Duties of the Local Ordinary Regarding Congregations of Women Religious of Pontifical Approval, V-195 pp., 1941.
129. Feeney, Rev. Thomas John, A.B., S.T.L., J.C.D., Restitutio in Integrum, VI-169 pp., 1941.

130. Findlay, Rev. Stephen William, O.S.B., A.B., J.C.D., Canonical Norms Governing the Deposition and Degradation of Clerics, XVII-279 pp., 1941.
131. Goodwine, Rev. John, A.B., S.T.L., J.C.D., The Right of the Church to Acquire Property, VIII-119 pp., 1941.
132. Heston, Rev. Edward Louis, C.S.C., Ph.D., S.T.D., J.C.D., The Alienation of Church Property in the United States, XII-222 pp., 1941.
133. Hogan, Rev. James John, A.B., S.T.L., J.C.D., Judicial Advocates and Procurators, XIII-200 pp., 1941.
134. Kealy, Rev. Thomas M., A.B., Litt.B., J.C.D., Dowry of Women Religious, IX-152 pp., 1941.
135. Keene, Rev. Michael James, O.S.B., J.C.D., Religious Ordinaries and Canon 198, V-164 pp., 1942.
136. Kerin, Rev. Charles A., S.S., M.A., S.T.B., J.C.D., The Privation of Christian Burial, XVI-279 pp., 1941.
137. Louis, Rev. William Francis, M.A., J.C.D., Diocesan Archives, X-101 pp., 1941.
138. McDevitt, Rev. Gilbert Joseph, A.B., J.C.D., Legitimacy and Legitimation, X-247 pp., 1941.
139. McDonough, Rev. Thomas Joseph, A.B., J.C.D., Apostolic Administrators, X-217 pp., 1941.
140. Meier, Rev. Carl Anthony, A.B., J.C.D., Penal Administrative Procedure Against Negligent Pastors, XI-240 pp., 1941.
141. Schmidt, Rev. John Rogg, A.B., J.C.D., The Principles of Authentic Interpretation in Canon 17 of the Code of Canon Law, XII-331 pp., 1941.
142. Slafkosky, Rev. Andrew Leonard, A.B., J.C.D., The Canonical Episcopal Visitation of the Diocese, X-197 pp., 1941.
143. Swoboda, Rev. Innocent Robert, O.F.M., J.C.D., Ignorance in Relation to the Imputability of Delicts, IX-271 pp., 1941.
144. Dube, Rev. Arthur Joseph, A.B., J.C.D., The General Principles for the Reckoning of Time in Canon Law, VIII-299 pp., 1941.
145. McBride, Rev. James T., A.B., J.C.D., Incardination and Excardination of Seculars, XX-585 pp., 1941.
146. Krol, Rev. John T., J.C.D., The Defendant in Contentious Trials, XII-207 pp., 1942.
147. Comyns, Rev. Joseph J., C.SS.R., A.B., J.C.D., Papal and Episcopal Administration of Church Property, XIV-155 pp., 1942.
148. Barry, Rev. Garrett Francis, O.M.I., J.C.D., Violation of the Cloister, XII-260 pp., 1942.
149. Bolduc, Rev. Gatien, C.S.V., A.B., S.T.L., J.C.D., Les Etudes dans les Religions Cléricales, VIII-155 pp., 1942.
150. Boyle, Rev. David John, M.A., J.C.D., The Juridic Effects of Moral Certitude on Pre-Nuptial Guarantees, XII-188 pp., 1942.

151. Canavan, Rev. Walter Joseph, M.A., Litt.D., J.C.D., The Profession of Faith, XII-143 pp., 1942.
152. Desrochers, Rev. Bruno, A.B., Ph.L., S.T.B., J.C.D., Le Premier Concile Plénier de Québec et le Code de Droit Canonique, XIV-186 pp., 1942.
153. Dillon, Rev. Robert Edward, A.B., J.C.D., Common Law Marriage, X-148 pp., 1942.
154. Dowell, Rev. Edward John, Ph.D., S.T.B., J.C.D., The Time and Place for the Celebration of Marriage, X-156 pp., 1942.
155. Donnellan, Rev. Thomas Andrew, A.B., J.C.D., The Obligation of the Missa pro Populo, VII-131 pp., 1942.
156. Eltz, Rev. Louis Anthony, A.B., J.C.D., Cooperation in Crime, XII-208 pp., 1942.
157. Gass, Rev. Sylvester Francis, M.A., J.C.D., Ecclesiastical Pensions, XI-206 pp., 1942.
158. Guiniven, Rev. John Joseph, C.SS.R., J.C.D., The Precept of Hearing Mass, XIV-188 pp., 1942.
159. Gulczynski, Rev. John Theophilus, J.C.D., The Desecration and Violation of Churches, X-126 pp., 1942.
160. Hammill, Rev. John Leo, M.A., J.C.D., The Obligations of the Traveler According to Canon 14, VIII-204 pp., 1942.
161. Haydt, Rev. John Joseph, A.B., J.C.D., Reserved Benefices, XI-148 pp., 1942.
162. Huser, Rev. Roger John, O.F.M., A.B., J.C.D., The Crime of Abortion in Canon Law, XII-187 pp., 1942.
163. Kearney, Rev. Francis Patrick, A.B., S.T.L., J.C.D., The Principles of Canon 1127, X-162 pp., 1942.
164. Linahen, Rev. Leo James, S.T.L., J.C.D., De Absolutione Complicis In Peccato Turpi, 114 pp., 1942.
165. McCloskey, Rev. Joseph Aloysius, A.B., J.C.D., The Subject of Ecclesiastical Law According to Canon 12, XVII-246 pp. 1942.
166. O'Neill, Rev. Francis Joseph, C.SS.R., J.C.D., The Dismissal of Religious in Temporary Vows, XIII-220 pp., 1942.
167. Prince, Rev. John Edward, A.B., S.T.B., J.C.D., The Diocesan Chancellor, X-136 pp., 1942.
168. Riesner, Rev. Albert Joseph, C.SS.R., J.C.D., Apostates and Fugitives from Religious Institutes, IX-168 pp., 1942.
169. Stenger, Rev. Joseph Bernard, J.C.D., The Mortgaging of Church Property, 186 pp., 1942.
170. Waldron, Rev. Joseph Francis, A.B., J.C.D., The Minister of Baptism, XII-197 pp., 1942.
171. Willett, Rev. Robert Albert, J.C.D., The Probative Value of Documents in Ecclesiastical Trials, X-124 pp., 1942.
172. Woeber, Rev. Edward Martin, M.A., J.C.D., The Interpellations, XII-161 pp., 1942.

173. Benko, Rev. Matthew Aloysius, O.S.B., M.A., J.C.D., The Abbot *Nullius,* XVI-148 pp., 1943.
174. Christ, Rev. Joseph James, M.A., S.T.L., J.C.D., Dispensation from Vindicative Penalties, XIV-285 pp., 1943.
175. Clancy, Rev. Patrick M. J., O.P., A.B., S.T.Lr., J.C.D., The Local Religious Superior, X-229 pp., 1943.
176. Clarke, Rev. Thomas James, J.C.D., Parish Societies, XII-147 pp., 1943.
177. Connolly, Rev. John Patrick, S.T.L., J.C.D., Synodal Examiners and Parish Priest Consultors, X-223 pp., 1943.
178. Drumm, Rev. William Martin, A.B., J.C.D., Hospital Chaplains, XII-175 pp., 1943.
179. Flanagan, Rev. Bernard Joseph, A.B., S.T.L., J.C.D., The Canonical Erection of Religious Houses, X-147 pp., 1943.
180. Kelleher, Rev. Stephen Joseph, A.B., S.T.B., J.C.D., Discussions with Non-Catholics: Canonical Legislation, X-93 pp., 1943.
181. Lewis, Rev. Gordian, C.P., J.C.D., Chapters in Religious Institutes, XII-169 pp., 1943.
182. Marx, Rev. Adolph, J.C.D., The Declaration of Nullity of Marriages Contracted Outside the Church, X-151 pp., 1943.
183. Matulenas, Rev. Raymond Anthony, O.S.B., A.B., J.C.D., Communication, a Source of Privileges, XII-225 pp., 1943.
184. O'Leary, Rev. Charles Gerard, C.SS.R., J.C.D., Religious Dismissed After Perpetual Profession, X-213 pp., 1943.
185. Power, Rev. Cornelius Michael, J.C.D., The Blessing of Cemeteries, XII-231 pp., 1943.
186. Shuhler, Rev. Ralph Vincent, O.S.A., J.C.D., Privileges of Regulars to Absolve and Dispense, XII-195 pp., 1943.
187. Ziolkowski, Rev. Thaddeus Stanislaus, A.B., J.C.D., The Consecration and Blessing of Churches, XII-151 pp., 1943.
188. Heneghan, Rev. John Joseph, S.T.D., J.C.D., The Marriages of Unworthy Catholics: Canons 1065 and 1066, XVI-213 pp., 1944.
189. Carroll, Rev. Coleman Francis, M.A., S.T.L., J.C.L., Charitable Institutions.
190. Ciesluk, Rev. Joseph Edward, Ph.B., S.T.L., J.C.D., National Parishes in the United States, VI-178 pp., 1944.
191. Coburn, Rev. Vincent Paul, A.B., J.C.D., Marriages of Conscience, XII-172 pp., 1944.
192. Connors, Rev. Charles Paul, C.S.Sp., A.B., J.C.D., Extra-Judicial Procurators in the Code of Canon Law, X-94 pp., 1944.
193. Coyle, Rev. Paul Raymond, A.B., J.C.D., Judicial Exceptions, X-142 pp., 1944.
194. Fair, Rev. Bartholomew Francis, A.B., S.T.L., J.C.D., The Impediment of Abduction, XII-122 pp., 1944.

195. GALLAGHER, REV. THOMAS RAPHAEL, O.P., A.B., S.T.Lr., J.C.D., The Examination of the Qualities of the Ordinand, X-166 pp., 1944.
196. GANNON, REV. JOHN MARK, S.T.L., J.C.D., The Interstices Required for the Promotion to Orders, XII-100 pp., 1944.
197. GOLDSMITH, REV. J. WILLIAM, B.C.S., S.T.L., J.C.D., The Competence of Church and State over Marriage—Disputed Points, X-128 pp., 1944.
198. GOODWINE, REV. JOSEPH GERARD, A.B., S.T.B., J.C.D., The Reception of Converts, XIV-326 pp., 1944.
199. KOWALSKI, REV. ROMUALD EUGENE, O.F.M., A.B., J.C.D., Sustenance of Religious Houses of Regulars, X-174 pp., 1944.
200. MCCOY, REV. ALAN EDWARD, O.F.M., J.C.D., Force and Fear in Relation to Delictual Imputability and Penal Responsibility, XII-160 pp., 1944.
201. MCDEVITT, REV. VINCENT JOHN, Ph.B., S.T.L., J.C.L., Perjury.
202. MARTIN, REV. THOMAS OWEN, Ph.D., S.T.D., J.C.D., Adverse Possession, Prescription and Limitation of Actions: The Canonical "Praescriptio," XX-208 pp., 1944.
203. MIKLOSOVIC, REV. PAUL JOHN, A.B., J.C.L., Attempted Marriages and Their Consequent Juridic Effects.
204. MUNDY, REV. THOMAS MAURICE, A.B., S.T.L., J.C.D., The Union of Parishes, X-164 pp., 1944.
205. O'DEA, REV. JOHN COYLE, A.B., J.C.D., The Matrimonial Impediment of Nonage, VIII-126 pp., 1944.
206. OLALIA, REV. ALEXANDER AYSON, S.T.L., J.C.D., A Comparative Study of the Christian Constitution of States and the Constitution of the Philippine Commonwealth, XII-136 pp., 1944.
207. POISSON, REV. PIERRE-MARIE, C.S.C., A.B., Ph.L., Th.L., J.C.L., Droits Patrimoniaux des Maisons et des Eglises Religieuses.
208. STADALNIKAS, REV. CASIMIR JOSEPH, M.I.C., J.C.D., Reservation of Censures, X-141 pp., 1944.
209. SULLIVAN, REV. EUGENE HENRY, S.T.L., J.C.D., Proof of the Reception of the Sacraments, X-165 pp., 1944.
210. VAUGHAN, REV. WILLIAM EDWARD, J.C.D., Constitutions for Diocesan Courts, X-210 pp., 1944.
211. PARO, REV. GINO, S.T.D., J.C.L., The Right of Apostolic Legation.
212. BALZER, REV. RALPH FRANCIS, C.P., J.C.D., The Computation of Time in a Canonical Novitiate, X-227 pp., 1945.
213. DOUGHERTY, REV. JOHN WHELAN, A.B., S.T.L., J.C.D., De Inquisitione Speciali, XII-195 pp., 1945.
214. DZIOB, REV. MICHAEL WALTER, J.C.D., The Sacred Congregation for the Oriental Church, XII-181 pp., 1945.
215. EIDENSCHINK, REV. JOHN ALBERT, O.S.B., B.A., J.C.D., The Election of Bishops in the Letters of Pope Gregory the Great, VII-200 pp., 1945.
216. GILL, REV. NICHOLAS, C.P., J.C.D., The Spiritual Prefect in Clerical Religious Houses of Study, X-140 pp., 1945.

217. Hynes, Rev. Harry Gerard, S.T.L., J.C.D., The Privileges of Cardinals, XII-183 pp., 1945.
218. McDevitt, Rev. Gerald Vincent, S.T.L., J.C.D., The Renunciation of an Ecclesiastical Office, XIV-179 pp., 1945.
219. Manning, Rev. Joseph Leroy, J.C.D., The Free Conferral of Offices, VIII-116 pp., 1945.
220. Meyer, Rev. Louis G., O.S.B., A.B., S.T.B., J.C.D., Alms-Gathering by Religious, XII-163 pp., 1945.
221. O'Donnell, Rev. Cletus Francis, M.A., J.C.D., The Marriage of Minors, XII-268 pp., 1945.
222. Prunskis, Rev. Joseph, J.C.D., Comparative Law, Ecclesiastical and Civil, in Lithuanian Concordat, X-161 pp., 1945.
223. Sweeney, Rev. Francis Patrick, C.SS.R., J.C.D., The Reduction of Clerics to the Lay State, X-199 pp., 1945.
224. Vogelpohl, Rev. Henry John, J.C.D., The Simple Impediments to Holy Orders, XVI-190 pp., 1945.
225. Brockhaus, Rev. Thomas Aquinas, O.S.B., A.B., J.C.D., Religious who Are Known as *Conversi*, X-127 pp., 1945.
226. Griese, Rev. N. Orville, S.T.D., J.C.D., The Marriage Contract and the Procreation of Offspring, XVI-224 pp., 1946.
227. Boudreaux, Rev. Warren Louis, J.C.L., The *"ab acatholicis nati"* of Canon 1099, § 2.
228. Bowe Rev. Thomas Joseph, A.B., J.C.D., Religious Superioresses, VIII-206 pp., 1946.
229. Diederichs, Rev. Michael Ferdinand, S.C.J., J.C.D., The Jurisdiction of the Latin Ordinaries over their Oriental Subjects, XIV-153 pp., 1946.
230. Dingman, Rev. Maurice John, A.B., S.T.L., J.C.L., The Plaintiff in Contentious Trials.
231. Frison, Rev. Basil, C.M.F., M.Mus., J.C.D., The Retroactivity of Law, X-221 pp., 1946.
232. Galvin, Rev. William Anthony, M.A., J.C.D., The Administrative Transfer of Pastors, XII-288 pp., 1946.
233. Goracy, Rev. Joseph C., J.C.L., The Diriment Matrimonial Impediment of Major Orders.
234. Hale, Rev. Joseph Francis, M.A., S.T.L., J.C.L., The Pastor of Burial.
235. Henry, Rev. Joseph Arthur, A.B., J.C.D., The Mass and Holy Communion: Inter-Ritual Law, XII-138 pp., 1946.
236. Linenberger, Rev. Herbert, C.PP.S., J.C.L., The False Denunciation of an Innocent Confessor.
237. Lowry, Rev. James Martin, A.B., J.C.D., Dispensation from Private Vows, XII-266 pp., 1946.
238. Lynch, Rev. George Edward, A.B., S.T.L., J.C.D., Coadjutors and Auxiliaries of Bishops, X-107 pp., 1947.

239. LYNCH, REV. TIMOTHY, M.S.SS.T., J.C.D., Contracts between Bishops and Religious Congregations, XIV-232 pp., 1946.
240. McCLUNN, REV. JUSTIN DAVID, A.B., S.T.L., J.C.D., Administrative Recourse, VII-142 pp., 1946.
241. LOHMULLER, REV. MARTIN NICHOLAS, A.B., J.C.D., The Promulgation of Law, XII-140 pp., 1947.
242. McGRATH, REV. JAMES, A.B., J.C.D., The Privilege of the Canon, XII-156 pp., 1946.
243. MARBACH, REV. JOSEPH FRANCIS, A.B., J.C.D., Marriage Legislation for the Catholics of the Oriental Rites in the United States and Canada, XIV-314 pp., 1946.
244. SHIMKUS, REV. BERNARD ALOYSIUS, A.B., J.C.L., The Determination and Transfer of Rite.
245. SMITH, REV. VINCENT MICHAEL, A.B., S.T.L., J.C.L., Ignorance Affecting Matrimonial Consent.
246. WACHTRLE, REV. PAUL ANTHONY, A.B., J.C.L., The Baptism of the Children of Non-Catholics.
247. CROTTY, REV. MATTHEW MICHAEL, J.C.L., The Recipient of First Holy Communion.
248. EAGLETON, REV. GEORGE, J.C.L., The Quinquennial Faculties, Formula IV.
249. GIBBONS, REV. MARION LEO, C.M., J.C.L., Domicile of the Wife Unlawfully Separated from Her Husband.
250. KELLY, REV. BERNARD MATTHEW, S.T.L., J.C.D., The Functions Reserved to Pastors, IX-141 pp., 1947.
251. KILCULLEN, REV. THOMAS JOHN, LL.M., J.C.D., The Collegiate Moral Person as Party Litigant, X-150 pp., 1947.
252. LAFONTAINE, REV. GERMAINE JOSEPH, W.F., J.C.L., Relations Canoniques entre le Missionaire et Ses Superieurs.
253. LANE, REV. LORAS THOMAS, J.C.L.,. Matrimonial Procedure in Ordinary Court of Second Instance.
254. LOVER, REV. JAMES FRANCIS, C.Ss.R., J.C.L., The Master of Novices.
255. McNICHOLAS, REV. TIMOTHY JOSEPH, J.C.L., The *Septimae Manus* Witness.
256. MAROSITZ, REV. JOSEPH JOHN, M.S.C., J.C.L., Obligations and Privileges of Religious Promoted to the Episcopal or Cardinalitial Dignities.
257. MURPHY, REV. FRANCIS JOSEPH, J.C.L., Legislative Powers of the Provincial Council.
258. O'BRIEN, REV. ROMAEUS WILLIAM, O.Carm., J.C.L., The Provincial Superior in Religious Orders of Men.
259. PFALLER, REV. BENEDICT ANTHONY, O.S.B., J.C.L., *The ipso facto* Effected Dismissal of Religious.
260. POPEK, REV. ALPHONSE SYLVESTER, J.C.L., The Rights and Obligations of Metropolitans.

261. Ristuccia, Rev. Bernard Joseph, C.M., J.C.L., Quasi-Religious.
262. Sonntag, Rev. Nathaniel Louis, O.F.M.Cap., J.C.L., Censorship of Special Classes of Books.
263. Stadler, Rev. Joseph Nicholas, J.C.L., Frequent Holy Communion.
264. Szal, Rev. Ignatius Joseph, J.C.L., The Communication of Catholics with Schismatics.
265. Wagner, Rev. Urban Stanley, O.F.M.Conv., J.C.D., Parochial Substitute Vicars and Supplying Priests, IX-126 pp., 1947.
266. Quinn, Rev. Joseph, M.A., J.C.L., Documents Required for the Reception of Orders.
267. Bennington, Rev. James Clement, A.B., J.C.L., The Recipient of Confirmation.
268. Blaher, Rev. Damian Joseph, O.F.M., A.B., J.C.L., The Ordinary Processes in Causes of Beatification and Canonization.
269. Clune, Rev. Robert Bell, B.A., J.C.L., The Judicial Interrogation of the Parties.
270. Courtemanche, Rev. Basil F., B.A., J.C.L., The Total Simulation of Matrimonial Consent.
271. Dlouhy, Rev. Maur John, O.S.B., A.B., J.C.L., The Ordination of Exempt Religious.
272. Donovan, Rev. John Thomas, Ph.B., S.T.L., J.C.L., The Clerical Obligations of Canons 138 and 140.
273. Freking, Rev. Frederick W., A.B., S.T.B., J.C.L., The Canonical Installations of Pastors.
274. Fulton, Rev. Thomas B., J.C.L., Prenuptial Investigation.
275. Godley, Rev. James P., J.C.L., The Time and the Place for the Celebration of Mass.
276. Kane, Rev. Thomas A., A.B., B.S., J.C.L., Jurisdiction of Patriarchs until 1439.
277. Kennedy, Rev. Andrew A., J.C.L., The Annual Pastoral Report to the Local Ordinary.
278. Konrad, Rev. Joseph George, J.C.L., Transfer of Religious.
279. Kress, Rev. Alphonse, J.C.L., Contumacy in Ecclesiastical Trials.
280. McCartney, Rev. Marcellus Anthony, O.F.M., M.A., J.C.L., Faculties of Regular Confessors.
281. McCaslin, Rev. Edward Patrick, M.A., S.T.L., J.C.L., The Division of Parishes.
282. McElroy, Rev. Francis J., A.B., J.C.L., The Privileges of Bishops.
283. Quinn, Rev. Stephen, M.S.SS.T., J.C.L., Relations between the Local Ordinary and Religious of Diocesan Approval.
284. Schneider, Rev. Edelhard Louis, S.D.S., M.A., J.C.D., The Status of Secularized Ex-Religious Clerics, x-155 pp., 1948.
285. Thompson, Rev. Chester J., A.B., J.C.L., The Simple Removal from Office.
286. O'Brien, Rev. Kenneth R., A.B., J.C.L., The Nature of Support of Diocesan Priests in the United States.

www.ingramcontent.com/pod-product-compliance
Lightning Source LLC
LaVergne TN
LVHW050230080826
844660LV00012B/506

* 9 7 8 0 8 1 3 2 2 4 6 2 6 *